Frances I Kershaw

**The gamekeeper's little son : and other stories for children**

Frances I Kershaw

**The gamekeeper's little son : and other stories for children**

ISBN/EAN: 9783741191794

Manufactured in Europe, USA, Canada, Australia, Japa

Cover: Foto ©Andreas Hilbeck / pixelio.de

Manufactured and distributed by brebook publishing software (www.brebook.com)

Frances I Kershaw

**The gamekeeper's little son : and other stories for children**

## Contents.

|  | PAGE |
|---|---|
| SIX LITTLE SISTERS | 108 |

"OLD CLO'ES":

| CHAPTER | |
|---|---|
| I. HIMSELF | 111 |
| II. A BUNDLE OF OLD CLOTHES | 116 |
| III. THE ACCIDENT | 131 |
| IV. LOTTY'S LARNIN' | 144 |
| V. ST. MARY'S CATECHISM CLASS | 152 |
| VI. LITTLE NELL'S BIRTHDAY | 160 |
| VII. VERY ILL | 169 |
| VIII. LITTLE NELL'S MOTHER | 183 |

# LITTLE ONES.

LITTLE ones! little ones!
  With eyes of brightest blue,
  Like the cloud above you—
    Guess how much we love you!
There's a nest in yon green tree—
Little robins one, two, three—
Little robins two, three, four:
Than mother-bird we love you more—
    Guess how much we love you!

Little ones! little ones!
  With faces sweetly fair,
  And clouds of golden hair—
    Guess how much we love you!

Little flowers love the dew—
Kiss it with their bright lips too:
More than theirs our love for you—
   Guess how much we love you!

Little ones! little ones!
Our love is yet more true
Than love of flower for dew—
   You know not how we love you!
Robin loves her birdlings four,
But our love for you is more:
Love alone can learn Love's lore—
   More than all, we love you!

# THE GAMEKEEPER'S LITTLE SON.

## CHAPTER I.

### OUR LITTLE HERO.

IT is drawing on towards evening. The shadows from the trees in the hedge are growing very long and dark on the road. The old village church looks dull and heavy, and its grey tower rises grimly out of the ivy that clings so closely round its lower half.

Close beside the church stands the gamekeeper's snug little cottage—so close that the churchyard path makes a nice short-cut to Birkham Woods, where the keeper's work lies. You can just see the woods now from the cottage, but they look very dim and blue in the twilight.

Inside the cottage it is darker still. Rows of fine geraniums and petunias in the window shut out what little light *would* come in if it only had a chance. But we must not say anything against the flowers, for they are Mrs. Graham's pride, and they won a first prize at the last show.

By the ruddy glow of the fire we can get a peep at the cozy party within. The strong, tall gamekeeper is sitting behind the petunias cleaning his gun. He is a fine, handsome fellow, but his hair has just begun to have a tinge of grey about it, and he has a great scar on his forehead. I think Graham is quite as proud of that scar as his wife is of her geraniums. He got it in a grand tussle with the poachers in Birkham Woods.

Mrs. Graham is sitting by the fireside, rocking to and fro in her arm-chair, and knitting away busily. On a three-legged stool beside her sits a little boy. A *very* little boy he is, so small that you would reckon his age to be seven at the very outside; but, nevertheless, Robin Graham has spent ten birthdays, with a plum-pudding on each of them, since he came into the world—not counting the first, which his father and mother kept for him with a great deal of thankfulness instead of the pudding !

Robin's face, what little there is of it, is more like a girl's than a boy's. It is a pale, delicate little face, with a pair of wistful brown eyes, and with straight brown hair parted over the middle of his forehead.

Some people say that Robin must have been a mistake for a girl; but I can't think that he is a mistake, after all. A very big, brave spirit—one that will do and dare, that will never stoop to a lie or a meanness of any sort—dwells in that frail, weakly body; and when you come to think of it, it is not really the *outside* of a person that matters so very much, but his *inside*. And Robin's inside is all right.

Presently Graham hangs his gun, bright and shining, across some hooks that run along the ceiling. His day's work is not ended yet, like most people's, but he can spare time to rest a bit. He goes to the window, and takes a peep out over his wife's flowers.

"That cat's there again, Robin," he says. "If I'd my gun loaded, it 'ud be for the last time too! It's my belief that she's carrying off a lev'ret in her mouth, the vixen!"

"I'll have her, father!" cries Robin, overturning the three-legged stool, and darting out into the twilight.

"Hist, puss!"

Away goes a large white cat across the little garden, her green eyes gleaming like two emeralds; and away goes Robin after her. He shies a few stones at her tail, but puss never heeds them, and finally disappears over the churchyard wall, tail and all!

Robin stops a moment. The wall is too high and too straight to climb, but he does not mean to give up the chase so easily.

Round by the gate he goes, just in time to see that tantalizing white tail give a last whisk behind a gravestone. Off darts Robin again in hot pursuit, but he sees no more of puss, until at length he hears a rustling amongst the ivy on the tower, and his sharp eyes spy out Miss Puss *just* disappearing through the belfry window with the leveret in her mouth.

Robin stands still to watch until even the tip of her tail is gone, and then he goes thoughtfully down the churchyard path towards home. He has something to think about. What *can* puss be doing up there? *How* did she get there? *Why* did she go there?

Thud! thud! thud!

Robin stands still to listen. There is a spade going somewhere, but nobody is to be seen.

Thud! thud!

Robin leaves the path, and goes in the direction of the sound. Suddenly a voice calls out, almost from under his very feet:

'Did you catch her, then, little 'un?"

"Who?" asks Robin, looking down into a deep grave, whence the voice seems to come. The voice itself belongs to the gravedigger, who is down in it.

"Tib—that white cat you were after just now."

"Oh, it's *you*, Mr. Berry!" exclaims Robin. "I didn't know who it was a bit, and I can't see you down there. So the white cat is called Tib, is she? No, I didn't anything like catch her; she can run so fast. Why, she was up that tower in no time, and there isn't no ladder nor nothing!"

"And you wouldn't want a ladder nor nothing neither, if you had *claws*, I reckon," answers Mr. Berry out of the dark grave. "It's her *claws* as does it, and her *mind* together. She's a very wise cat, is Tib! I never knowed a little boy catch her yet."

"How do you know her name *is* Tib, Mr. Berry?" asks Robin.

"Well, I suppose because I christened her. She knows her own name, anyway. You just see. Tib! Tib!"

"Me-ow." Up at the entrance to the belfry window appears the white cat's head and her green eyes.

"Good Tib! poor old Tib!" says the gravedigger; and Tib disappears again.

"Well, now, that's perfectly wonderful!" cries Robin. "How ever did you get to know her so well, Mr. Berry?"

"Ah! well, that's a secret, you see," says the gravedigger very mysteriously. "And if I were to tell *you*, it wouldn't be a secret any longer, I suppose. How did you get to know your mother so well, little Robin?"

"Well, I don't know," Robin answers thoughtfully. He has never put the question to himself before. "Maybe it's because mother keeps that a secret too."

"She's a very wonderful woman, is *your mother*, Robin—mind *that!*" says the gravedigger solemnly.

"Yes," nods Robin back, "she is, very. I don't suppose anybody's got a wonderfuller mother than mine."

"Mine was a wonderful woman too, Robin —a very wonderful woman —afore I buried her."

"I shouldn't like having to bury my

mother," says Robin. "I think I'd rather die first, and have somebody else to bury us both. Mr. Berry!"

"Well, Robin?"

"Father's going to shoot that cat—he says so! It's going off with all the young rabbits."

"You just tell your father from me, Robin, that if he wants to kill white Tib, he'll have to shoot me first."

"He'd never do *that*, Mr. Berry," says Robin. "He thinks a deal too much of you and Mrs. Berry; and besides, he'd get took up if he did."

"And hanged; an' I'd have to bury him. He'd take a fine big grave, would your father, Robin!"

"But how could you bury him if you was shot, Mr. Berry?" asks Robin.

The gravedigger does not answer his question, but only keeps throwing up shovelful after shovelful of earth, with the thud that Robin heard before.

His work is done at last. He sticks his

great spade into the heap of earth at the top of the grave, and is up by Robin's side in a moment.

"I guess you're waiting for me to go home with you, ain't you, Robin?" he says. "I never knowed a little lad as liked to pass through a churchyard 'cept i' the daylight, 'cause of the ghos'es—more especially a poor little scared-looking lad like you. Come on, then."

"I wasn't waiting for that," says Robin simply. "I've been here often and often in the dark; I'm not afraid. I've been stayin' to think."

"And what had *you* to think about, little Robin?"

"Lots of things," answers Robin; "but most about cats and graves just then. I didn't stop 'cos I was *afraid*, Mr. Berry."

"Why, you look as if you were never nought *but* afraid, Robin," says the gravedigger good-naturedly. "You'll never be a fit man to meet the poachers, like your father!"

## The Gamekeeper's Little Son.

"No," answers Robin, with a little sigh; "never."

"I guess you'd never be able to do as much as my cat—climb up into that there belfry tower—would you?"

"I'll tell you what, Mr. Berry, I mean to *try*," answers Robin decidedly. "And if I can do *that*, you'll not go for to call me 'scared' and 'little' again, will you, Mr. Berry?"

"Well, if ever you *do* manage such a thing with your neck whole, I reckon I'll have enough to do *lookin'* at you, without so much as a word. Good-bye, Robin; and mind I see you some of these days with your brown eyes beside Tib's green ones in the belfry. Which'll shine brightest, eh?"

Robin only gives a knowing little nod, and goes in to tell his father about the wonderful white cat in the belfry.

## CHAPTER II.

#### A SUCCESSFUL ATTEMPT.

"Mr. Berry, please."

"Well, Robin; what now?"

"Mr. Berry, what have you got in that nice little tin—your dinner?"

"Somebody *else's*," says the gravedigger, shaking his head mysteriously.

"Whose?" asks Robin; "there isn't nobody here but you and me, and I've had my dinner a great while ago."

"It's a secret, Robin; a very particular secret!"

"But I don't like secrets," says Robin; "except when I make 'em myself, and then I always know 'em."

"You're like a many other folks," says old Berry. "May be I'll tell you about *my* secret when you're as good a hand at climbing as my white Tib. There she goes up the ivy! Ain't she sharp about it? When'll you be able to do *that*, little Robin?"

"'Little' again!" mutters Robin, with a deep sigh. "She's *ever* so much littler, is Tib. I'll tell you what, Mr. Berry, I'll go and have a try at that tower now; and I'll never stop trying till I can get up as quick as white Tib."

But the gravedigger only shakes his white head, and rests awhile on his spade to watch little Robin, who is trying hard to find a footing on the old ivied tower.

Robin tumbles down so many times that at last Mr. Berry grows tired of looking at him, and begins to ply his spade again busily.

In about an hour's time, when the old man has forgotten all about little Robin Graham, and all about everything else except the work he is intent upon completing before nightfall, he is startled by hearing his own name repeated very distinctly many times.

"Mr. Berry! Hey, Mr. Berry!"

The gravedigger stares about him far and wide, but cannot tell where the voice comes from.

Then white Tib rushes past, with her tail flying and her eyes shining.

"Why, whatever's frightened the cat!" mutters the old man. "Sure*ly* that young squit of a child's never——"

For very amazement, Mr. Berry never puts an end to that sentence. Up in the belfry-window, between the ivy-sprays, where the white cat usually sits, is perched little Robin Graham, looking down very triumphantly upon the old man.

"You won't never call me 'little' again now, you know!" he shouts. "You promised you wouldn't, Mr. Berry."

"Well, if I ever did see such a owdacious young creetur' in all *my* born days—let alone those of other people! However did you get up there, Robin? You've given Tib such a scare!"

"I got hard hold of the ivy," says Robin proudly, "and pulled myself up in the same way as Tib—though I *haven't* claws to help me! And I mean to practise every day till I can climb every bit as fast as she does. Now, you said you would tell me what that stuff in your tin is for, if I got up here."

"Well, it's for Tib, if you must know," says the gravedigger. "It's some milk as my missus sets by for her, and I take it up the belfry-ladder, and leave it in her window for her. Maybe you'll like to give her this, to make up for the scaring. Come down and fetch it, then."

Robin is thinking of making his way down by the ivy, as he came up, but the old man will not hear of such a thing.

"Come down by the belfry-ladder, Robin," he says, "and I'll unlock the tower-door for you. You'll only break your neck the other way. It's not worth much, to be sure; but you'd make me a sight more work in the gravedigging line, since you've growed so big all of a sudden."

There is a twinkle in his eyes as he speaks.

Robin makes his way down the dusty ladder, and has Tib's little tin of milk given into his care. But nothing will induce Robin to go up again that way. He manages to climb the ivy once more, with the tin in his mouth, held tightly between clenched teeth, and lands himself and it safely on the belfry window-seat.

Tib is nowhere to be seen; so Robin fills her saucer, and comes down once more by the ladder.

Old Berry has by this time finished his work, and is just starting homewards. Robin goes with him to the church-gate, and there they say good-night to each other.

Never a word does Robin say at home of that day's clever deed, though you may be sure his thoughts are all running upon it. When he can climb as well as white Tib, *then*, he thinks, will be time enough to let the world know of it.

Little does Robin Graham think that, before very long, his climbing will stand him in good stead!

## CHAPTER III.

#### ROBIN'S ERRAND.

"ROBIN," says the gamekeeper one afternoon, "do you think I can trust you to run a very important errand for me?"

Robin's truthful eyes look straight up into his father's face, and he says, smiling:

"*Of course* you can, father!"

"Well, then, my boy, take the message I am going to give you straight to Mr. Woods, the keeper at Markham. Don't forget a word; and mind you don't leave it with anybody but himself. Bid him be ready in Birkham Woods to-morrow night by eight o'clock, at the place where the pheasants feed, with as many men as he can gather, and as many stout sticks. Tell him I've heard to-day that there's something up among those poaching fellows, and I mean to be too much for 'em this time. Mind you tell him right, Robin."

"Yes, father; I'll mind," says Robin.

"Oh, Herbert!" says Robin's mother, looking up from her work anxiously; "I can't a-bear to hear of those frays you're having with the poachers. I'd rather see them clear the woods of every creature that's in 'em than have you put your life in such danger. When you've got a wife and child to see to I don't think it's a right thing; I don't, indeed!"

"Never you fear, mother," her husband answers good-humouredly; "Robin'll take care of me, if need be; won't you, Robin?"

"If I could I would, father," Robin says sadly; "but then folks says I'm so little, and always shall be. Eh, father! I would like to be strong and big, and go and thrash the poachers along with you."

"Never you mind what folks says, Robin," says Graham, stroking the soft straight hair off Robin's forehead. "Folks *will* say. You're every bit big and strong enough for me and mother, lad."

"And mind, Robin," adds his mother, "there's

many a finer thing in the world than fighting a bad lot of poachers!"

"Good-bye, mother and Robin," says the keeper, going out with his gun. "I'm going myself into the village to seek up some other men to stand by us if need be. Mind you don't forget my message, lad!"

"I'll not forget a word, father."

And Robin takes his cap down from its peg, and trots off, past the little garden and the churchyard, on towards Birkham Woods, through which his way lies.

He passes the gravedigger's snug cottage, where Mrs. Berry sits knitting busily in the doorway, with the white cat curled up in a ball at her feet, purring briskly to keep time with the click of the needles. Good Mrs. Berry always has a nod and a smile ready for Robin when he passes. He is a great favourite of hers. She has never had a little boy of her own, so she and Mrs. Graham go shares in the matter of Robin, and that is next best.

The white cat is never "scared" at Robin now. They are the very best of friends.

Robin's brown eyes, as the old gravedigger once said in fun, are often to be seen by the side of Tib's green ones in the belfry-window.

Markham lies a good long way from Robin's home, and so, by the time the little boy has carried his father's message safely to the keeper, it is beginning to grow quite late.

And as Robin's legs are very short, and very soon tired, it is later still when he reaches the woods once more.

The sun has given his last sly wink over the horizon, before going to bed, some time ago. The moon is not up yet; so it is beginning to get really dusk outside the woods, and *very* dark inside them.

Robin doesn't quite fancy the great black shadows that lie across his path, the strange noise of the wind in the trees, and the stillness of everything else all around him. But, as I said before, Robin's is a brave little heart; so he plucks up courage, and trots steadily on over the soft moss.

Something, too, that his father once told him when he was afraid of the dark comes into Robin's mind now. It was about those kind, good angels who stay in our dreary world just on purpose to take care of little boys like Robin, who cannot take care of themselves.

"And it doesn't make a bit of matter to 'em," thinks Robin, "whether it's dark or light. I reckon they're like our Tib, something, in their eyes—she *can* see in the dark! Why, I shouldn't wonder if all those white things movin' in the woods ain't angels!"

And the thought of the angels comforts Robin nicely, and makes a sort of backbone to his courage.

And so Robin and his thoughts go on together until he reaches the place where the pheasants feed.

"They'll be here to-morrow night, I s'pose," he says to himself. "I wonder what'll happen!"

Then, with a little sigh, "Eh, if I was only big and strong to go along with father and meet 'em! It's very sad for people when they can't help bein' so little! Hark! what is that?"

It is a sound not often heard in Birkham Woods at that time of night—a gun going off.

"Why, it's father!" thinks Robin at first. "Whatever can bring father here at this time of night?"

But then comes a thought that frightens the little boy left all alone in the dark woods.

It may be *the poachers!*

Robin trembles, and holds his breath as he thinks of it.

The Birkham poachers are such an awfully bold, wicked lot of men. Robin feels sure that they will do him some harm if they find him, and think that he is playing the spy upon them.

The gun goes off again—quite close to Robin this time. He hears something fall heavily to the ground, and then catches sight of a dark figure stooping down to pick up what has fallen.

Robin himself is safely hidden by the shadow of an oak. By-and-by other men come up, and Robin hears about half a dozen of them talking to one another in low voices. He can only catch a few broken bits of what they say, but what he does hear is enough to prove to him that they are poachers, and up to no good.

"What's kep' the man so late?" says one.

"He'll miss the peppering we've got ready for him," says another.

"And that would be such a pity, after all our trouble!" says a third.

"He'll not miss it, if I have to hang for it," mutters the first man. "I'm not quits with him yet about that thrashing he gived our Joe."

"Graham'll die hard," adds another. "We'll maybe feel his hand first, some on us!"

"Getting chicken-hearted?" sneers the first man.

"Not I! It's me you have to thank for laying this fine plot, Stalker; so none of your chaff! If I hadn't done the old fellow by giving him to understand that I'd help him to set you all in gaol to-morrow night, and got him to promise to send word to Woods, where'd you all be to-night, I'd like to know ?"

Then the men draw close to one another, and speak in still lower voices.

Poor little Robin stands trembling in the shade, and knows not what to do.

It is clear that the poachers are not only aware of his father's plans, but that they have laid a terrible plot against him.

How is Robin to prevent his father from falling into the snare ? He knows well that ere a few moments have passed, it will be too late. The gamekeeper will have set off on his nightly rounds through the woods. And what will happen *then*, Robin trembles to think. What shall he do ?

Robin's mind is made up, and there is no time to be lost. Bravely he dashes out of the oak shade, and flies along the path homewards with the speed of a hunted hare.

He is too late. The poachers' sharp ears, awake to the faintest sound, hear the rustling of the trees as he passes, and the light fall of his feet on the moss.

"There are spies at work!" cries one angrily. "The worse for them, that's all!" And away he dashes after the poor little frightened boy, followed by all his comrades.

## CHAPTER IV.

#### A TERRIBLE NIGHT.

MRS. BERRY is busy closing her window-shutters for the night—sweet, balmy summer evening as it is. She and her old husband always shut up the house early, and spend the twilight hours chatting over their cosy fire.

"Hark! what is that?" mutters the good woman, standing still with a shutter in her hand to listen.

She hears the sound of many heavy feet crossing the road over against her cottage. Then, a moment after, she sees a little panting, breathless figure hurry past her door, and dash into the churchyard through the open gate.

The moon is shining brightly now, and Mrs. Berry recognises, to her astonishment, that the little fugitive is none other than Robin Graham.

"Whatever can have scared the dear little lad?" she mutters to herself, as she fastens the cross-bar of the shutter. "It 'ud take a deal to scare him like that!"

Before the good woman can think of any possible answer to her question, half a dozen rough men dash past her, and through the gate into the churchyard.

"Mercy on us! whatever's up?" exclaims Mrs. Berry. "It's the poachers! Now, the saints and angels keep my little Robin, for they've some spite against him, for certain."

Mrs. Berry hurries into the kitchen to give her old husband an account of what is going on.

Mr. Berry is comfortably settled in his chair by the fire, reading his paper and puffing away at a clay pipe between whiles. He looks up as his wife enters the cottage.

"Whatever's up now, Becky? You're about the colour o' one o' your own clean-washed sheets! What's given you a turn, lass?"

"Oh, that poor, dear, little lad!" groans Mrs. Berry, sinking into a chair. "It's little Robin Graham, you know, Caleb. I see'd him go by this afternoon, with his bright little face, and he stooped down and stroked our white Tib. And just now, as I shut up the shutters, he comes flying past like the wind of a winter's night, with a lot of men at his heels. Poachers they was, I know; for I'm certain I caught sight of Carter and Blake, and the rest of the set are never far apart. Oh, Caleb! what *shall* we do? I make no doubt but they're after some harm with the poor little lad."

The good old gravedigger lays aside his pipe and paper, as his wife speaks, leaves his comfortable chair, and goes out with his trusty staff into the moonlight.

## A Terrible Night.

"I'm going to give Herbert Graham a word o' warnin'," he says. "I fancy the poachers are up to something, and he must have his eyes open. I'll maybe see something of the little lad on my way. Never you fear, Becky; surely they'd never hurt a child that could do 'em neither good nor harm! Leave the door on the latch, wife, if it's bed-time before I come back. It strikes me there'll be work to do to-night. And mind and say your prayers, Becky, for all of us!"

The old gravedigger has hardly reached Graham's cottage before poor Becky, saying her beads before the fire, with a beating heart, is startled by hearing loud knocks at her door —not once nor twice.

She has not time to open it before a lot of men burst in upon her, hot and angry.

"If thou'st got him in here, old dame," cries the foremost, "thou'st best give him up! We don't mean no harm to the chit; but he's been peeking and peering where he hadn't no business; and perhaps a word or two of wholesome warning'll help to keep his tongue still. So give him up quiet, and we won't make no row."

"There's never a body in the house but myself," stammers poor Becky, frightened out of her wits by the man's rough voice and manner. "Nor there hasn't been nobody come here. You may search the cottage through, if it pleases you."

"Ay, that we will, old dame!" cries one of the poachers. "It's pretty certain, to our minds, that he's somewhere round, and your cottage stands in the road oncommon handy."

While the men stamp with heavy feet through Betty's little home, searching even the chest where are kept the good woman's best bonnet and shawls, with Caleb's Sunday suit—of course, to no purpose—let us follow the fortunes of our little Robin.

When we heard of him last, he had just reached the churchyard in safety, and was running down the path to his father's gate, when he saw in the distance a dark figure crouching down behind a gravestone, as if lying in wait for him.

Poor Robin turned back with a terrible fright; wherever he might go, enemies seemed to lurk. In his terror he almost threw himself into the very arms of the poachers. But now, when his fate seems sealed, and escape impossible, Robin finds a friend to help him in his trouble.

"Me-ow!"

It is the dear old white cat. The poachers seem to have alarmed her as well as Robin. She flies across Robin's path like a tiny white ghost, up the ivied tower of the church, and disappears in an instant.

White Tib has put a grand idea into Robin's head: he will follow her example. Certainly there is nothing better to be done. Up the ivy he goes after white Tib, and its great boughs almost hide him from view. He is soon seated, safe and sound, but oh! so weary and frightened, beside his green-eyed friend.

It is just now, when Robin is safe in the belfry tower, that the poachers, having lost sight of him, hurry to Mrs. Berry's cottage, expecting to find him hidden there.

3—2

Perched up so high in the belfry window, Robin sees this, and gets a good view of all that is passing below. He sees old Caleb hobble down the path, and enter his father's cottage. He sees the figure of his mother at the door as she opens it, and the ruddy glow of the firelight within; then it is quickly closed again, and only the dreary twilight world outside to be seen.

Oh, how the little weary boy longs to be once more safe in that snug cottage, telling all his troubles as he nestles close to his mother's side! Father, too—oh, how he wants to tell father that he must not, *must not*, go on his rounds to-night; that the poachers have laid a terrible plot against him; that there is danger, perhaps even *death*, lying in wait for him! And yet here he must stay helplessly in the old church tower. If he were to leave it, it would be but to fall into the hands of the poachers.

White Tib is a comfort to poor Robin as he waits; and cat-comfort is well worth having when you can get no other. She curls herself

## A Terrible Night.

up on his shoulder, with her tail swung round his neck, and her head rubs gently against his face with a soft, soothing purr.

"I should like to comfort you, little Robin, if I could!" her purr seems to say.

"Poor Tib, how nice and kind you are!" Robin whispers gratefully, just as if puss could understand what he says. "I wonder if the angels ever climb up into belfry towers, Tib?"

"Purr! purr!"

"Yes, Tib, I suppose they do. Please, dear angel, take care of father! Go down to him, and never mind me!"

"Purr! purr!"

"*You* can't understand about it, Tib; I wish you could. You only care about being comfortable, and having your nice milk, and being able to catch birds and mice for your dinner, and rolling yourself up before Mrs. Berry's fire; and—well, yes, I believe you *do* care a little about *me!* But you can't *love*, Tib; that's quite a different thing. Cats can't do it. But I *do* love father; and oh, Tib, dear Tib, I'd rather let the poachers do anything they liked to *me* than have them hurt father!"

"Purr! purr!"

"Yes, Tib, you can purr," says Robin, with his eyes full of tears. "Please go on purring; I like to hear you."

The old church clock strikes the hour of eight, and the belfry trembles with each number.

"That's bed-time," says Robin. "Mother'll be waiting to give me her good-night kiss and blessing. Poor mother! I suppose I shan't go to bed to-night; I can say my night-prayers here, though."

And Robin has never said his prayers with so much heart in them before. It is wonderful how trouble brings us quite close to God, and makes speaking to Him so real and easy!

"Hark, puss! what is that noise?"

Puss pricks up her ears, and Robin looks down. Somebody is going quickly along the road and turning through the little gate that leads into the woods. Robin knows who it is at once; no one else in all Birkham is so tall and strong. It is his father—Herbert Graham. He is too far away for any voice to reach him.

"Oh, father, father!" moans poor little Robin, "you are going to the woods, I know, and the poachers will be there before you! Oh, father!" and Robin bursts into very bitter tears, which fall like dewdrops on to pussy's soft fur.

"Purr, purr!" says Tib, as she rubs her nose gently against his. "Purr, purr!"

"Poor puss!" says Robin sadly. "What shall we do?"

Once more puss pricks up her sharp ears, and Robin looks down. His father is out of sight, but old Caleb Berry is hobbling slowly up the churchyard path again. White Tib knows her master at once; she leaves her place in the belfry, creeps down the ivy, and goes to meet him.

Robin can't help giving a little cry of joy at the sight of his old friend, and then he follows pussy's example.

"Heyday!" exclaims the gravedigger, lifting up both hands at meeting Robin there at that time of night. "Whatever are you doing here, lad? Thy mother's fretting after thee sorely, Robin, and thy father has gone off to the woods to seek thee. 'Tain't no foolish trick you're playing, I hope, little Robin?"

"Oh, no," says Robin quickly; "it's the poachers. I've heard them in the woods to-day, saying they've laid a snare for father to-night. I tried to run and tell father before he started on his rounds, but they were after me, and I had only just time to climb up into the old tower. They're seeking me still in your cottage, Mr. Berry, but they'll soon go back to the woods, I know. Oh, what *shall* we do to save father?"

The old man looks very gravely at Robin for a moment, then he says:

"Robin, thou art a brave little lad, and thou lovest thy father. Look here, I'll bide in the house, and help those men to hunt for you there, while you run after your father and bring him back. You've time yet, for your mother said he'd started but just afore I got there. I'd go myself if I were ten years younger; but he'd be in their hands long afore my poor old legs could catch him up. Run your fastest, lad; and God speed you!"

Robin does not delay a moment. Long before the old gravedigger has reached his cottage-door, the nimble little feet are far on their way, and for a second time Robin enters the gloomy woods.

No moonlight shines through the thick shade of pine and oak to light up the winding paths, and poor little Robin stumbles over sticks and stumps many a time as he hurries on. He has forgotten how tired he is, poor child! His mind is full of his father, and how to save him; and his heart, as it beats so quickly, is breathing forth short, quick cries for help to the dear Mother of Mercy.

Robin is near the pheasants' feeding-place now; surely his father cannot be very far off. He hears footsteps ahead. No one is to be seen, for the shadows of the trees lie everywhere dark and thick; but Robin never doubts that it is father.

"Stop!" he whispers softly, "stop!"

The footsteps still move on; father has not heard.

"Stop—stop! the poachers!" cries Robin loudly, his voice hoarse with running; and the footsteps cease.

Robin hastens forward to whisper words of warning in his father's ear, when suddenly there is the loud report of a gun—the sound of something falling to the ground—heavy feet hurrying away; and then, no sound at all—only a terrible, dead silence!

## CHAPTER V.

### NEXT MORNING.

THERE is a light burning in Caleb Berry's cottage all through the night, and Caleb himself sits half-dozing over the dying embers of his fire. He cannot rest in bed to-night.

The old man is sorely troubled that his friend, Herbert Graham, has not yet returned safely. All that he could do to keep the poachers in the house until Robin should have had time to come up with his father was in vain. Perhaps they guessed by the old man's eagerness, and by his trembling voice, that something was up; anyway, soon after Robin set off they also left the cottage, and turned up the road to the woods.

White Tib seems restless too. She lays herself down at her master's feet for a few moments, then gets up again, and walks round and round the room, stopping every now and then as if to listen.

"Poor old Tib!" says the gravedigger, stroking her neck kindly. "Dost thou know aught of what's up, that thou canst not rest? Eh, but thou art a wise cat, Tib!"

"Me-ow!" answers white Tib, very mournfully.

"Poor little Robin!" says the gravedigger. "He was the only sort of bird thee ever took to, Tib. And his father was my friend, Tib;

but I always liked little Robin. We'll say a
'Hail Mary' for them both, Tib. Poor little
Robin!"

Old Berry has been many a time up and
down between Graham's cottage and his own,
with white Tib at his heels, to hear from the
poor, anxious mother whether she has heard
anything of her husband and Robin, but there
is no news all that night.

Early morning comes at last. The light of
day creeps in through the shutter-chinks, and
old Berry drags his stiffened limbs to the
window to open it and the shutters. As he
does so, even his deaf ears catch the sound of
something coming. Footsteps he makes out
the sound to be—how many feet he cannot
tell. White Tib hears them too, and purrs
loudly.

"Now God be praised!" he murmurs, "'tis
Graham come at last! Tib, it's the little lad
back again! Eh, but it's been a long, weary
night!"

By this time the feet have come nearer, and
Caleb, craning his neck out of the window,

can see that it is indeed his old friend. But where is Robin? Perhaps the little lad has run on before to get his mother's kiss.

Old Berry puts on his hat, once more takes his stick, and sallies forth to meet Graham with a welcome home. White Tib will not be left behind, and she follows him closely.

But Caleb's welcome is soon changed to a terrible fear. He meets Graham's sad, anxious face, and there, in Graham's arms, instead of the gun he generally carries—his own little son, Robin!

The little boy lies quite still in his father's arms; his legs hang limply down, and the red blood trickles down his face from a wound in his forehead, in spite of the handkerchief that binds it.

"You don't say *so!*" is all Caleb's trembling lips can whisper, and the tears chase one another down his honest old face. He loves little Robin as though he were his own child. "What's come to the bairn, Graham?"

"Thou shalt hear all I know after," says the keeper very mournfully. "But now, Caleb, will you go, like a friend, to prepare my wife? This mustn't come sudden-like on her."

"Ay," answers old Berry; and he hobbles away down the churchyard as fast as his feeble limbs and his trusty staff will take him.

Mrs. Graham is standing at her door, as she has stood ever since day dawned, with a pale, anxious face, eagerly straining her eyes now to make sure that it is indeed her own husband coming home at last.

She never sees the old gravedigger until he is quite close to her, and not then until he speaks; for, meantime, Graham has been slowly drawing nearer, and a sickening dread seizes her poor mother-heart as she catches sight of the little motionless burden in his arms.

"It's Caleb," she says. "You've come to tell me that something has happened. Don't be afraid to speak; tell me—I can bear anything!"

Then old Berry tells her very tenderly and carefully that an accident has happened, and she must get everything ready for her little wounded lad. He tries to speak words of comfort to her as best he can.

Mrs. Graham neither sobs nor faints. All her thought is with her little Robin. With a white, calm face she gets Robin's own little bed ready, and everything that she will want to dress the wound. She leaves herself no time to think about herself, and by-and-by, when Graham comes in, she is ready to take her boy from his arms, and to set him free to go for the surgeon.

All that long day and the next Robin spends in trying to struggle back to life; and turn by turn, the whole of that time, Mrs. Berry and his mother watch and pray over him.

Another friend, too, scarcely leaves Robin for a moment. Can you guess who it is? With her round green eyes peering over the bedclothes, and her soft purr breaking the silence of the room, sits the white cat, Tib. When Robin first opens his brown eyes wearily to the light, they meet the glassy green eyes of poor puss gazing at him with a wealth of pity and love in them.

But Robin will never again climb the old ivied tower with white Tib. That dreadful wound never heals—never!

A few short weeks after, if you go into the churchyard, you may see old Berry shovelling earth and tears into a little grave he has dug there. If you ask him whose it is, he will not be able to tell you for sobs; but come a few days later, and a little white tombstone stands at its head. You may read it for yourself—

ROBIN GRAHAM,

*Aged* 10 *Years.*

R. I. P.

And just underneath, something about being "faithful unto death."

The little robins, his namesakes, come here now and then, and sing little sad songs of their own, but nobody has ever yet been able to hear the words. And when the dusk of evening gathers round, a little white creature may be seen to come stealing down from the old belfry tower, and to curl itself up in the soft green grass that grows on that tiny grave, as if to keep guard.

White Tib does not know, you see, that little Robin Graham—brave, loving, faithful little soul!—is safe now for ever, somewhere higher far than the top of the belfry tower, even with the angels.

---

## CHAPTER VI.

### HOW THEY TALK ABOUT ROBIN.

It always makes them sad—oh, very!—but still they like to talk about it—how little Robin Graham, I mean, met his death in Birkham Woods. Listen to the old people now.

It is a pleasant summer evening—very, very still. The soft air is heavy with the perfume of the flowers from Graham's pretty, well-kept garden. Only from the distant woods comes the gentle cooing of the wood-pigeons as they sing soothing lullabies to their nestlings in the tree-tops. In the tiny garden the two old couples sit, talking in low, tender voices of the little lad whose quiet grave they see resting under the shadow of the ivied church-tower. White Tib is sitting at old Berry's feet; she almost seems to be listening to what they are saying about little Robin, but of course this is only fancy.

"Poor old Tib!" says the gravedigger sadly, "she's never been the same since our Robin died. It's a'most a miracle to hear her purr now—a thing she used scarce ever to stop doing."

"And she don't seem to care for her milk as she did when he took it to her in the tower, Caleb," adds Mrs. Berry; "nor for keeping her fur clean and beautiful, as she used. She's a changed cat, is Tib, since our Robin died!"

"Everything's changed," says the gamekeeper very mournfully, "since our Robin died; nothing looks the same. But I suppose it's a good thing, wife, after all; it makes you and me look *up* where we used to look *down*, perhaps, too much. And I don't think our prayers have grown worse since the little lad's been up there to help them."

And Mrs. Graham *looks* the words she can't trust her voice to say.

"Tell us all about it again, Herbert," says the gravedigger, as he has said it for fifty times at least. He knows that the keeper is never tired of speaking of Robin, any more than they are ever tired of hearing about him.

"You begin, Caleb," says his wife.

"Well, it was when I met the little lad in the churchyard; 'Robin,' I said, 'run and warn your father, and I'll try my best to keep the poachers back.' They were in my cottage then, and Herbert was off for the woods. Robin never waited a second bidding; you'd a' thought he had wings by how he flew."

"Ay, he *did* love his father, did Robin!" whispers Mrs. Graham.

Big tears are rolling slowly down the honest keeper's cheeks.

"But I couldn't hold the poachers back," Berry goes on sorrowfully. "They were off to the woods a'most directly; and there they waited by the pheasants' feeding-place to do their dark deed. Poor little Robin! he never guessed they'd be there before him; he was thinkin' only of his father. The first man he could make out in the darkness, thinks he, 'That's father,' and he whispers, 'Stop, stop!' but no one heard. Then he calls aloud, 'Stop, stop! the poachers!' That was his own death-cry. It was never his father, but the worst of the poachers, that wretched man *Stalker*."

"*Don't* say his name, Caleb!" Mrs. Graham entreats, shuddering.

"Well, they didn't make out whose the voice was, but they guessed it must be Graham's; so *he* fired in the dark, and at random, and there, without a cry or a groan, that innocent little lad was laid low. Then the wretch who had done the fell deed fled to join his comrades, and to make plans for preventing their crime coming to light."

## How they talk about Robin.

"Now you, Herbert," says Mrs. Berry.

The keeper dries his eyes, and speaks in very broken tones:

"I'd taken my way to the woods as usual that night. I thought as I went that I might meet little Robin. He was very late in coming home. He might have lost his way in the dark, so I took my lantern. You know how still it was that evening, Caleb! Never a breath of wind stirred, and the whole wood seemed for all the world like a dead thing. I'd passed the pheasants' feeding-place, seen that all was right, and was going further, when suddenly I heard the sound of a gun going off, and I stopped to make out what was up. Then there came the sound of feet running. I said to myself, 'It's poachers; the men must have got scent of our plans, and they mean to surprise us to-night. I'll go on at once to the Markham keeper, and get him to join me in nabbing some of these fellows. Once make an example of a few of them, and this poaching business is at an end. They are but cowards, at the best.' So I shaded my lantern with my hand, and went through the woods to Markham by that very path that poor little Robin had been by that very afternoon.

"I found the keeper at home, and he soon got a good stout gang of men together, with what weapons they could muster. We'd hardly entered the woods before we fell in with the band of poachers. They thought they had laid their enemy low for ever, and were making the best of their way out of the woods as far as possible from where they had entered it, that their footmarks might not betray them. We took them by surprise, and made most of them prisoners, that wretched man Stalker amongst them.

"Sullenly and silently we led them to the village lock-up, to spend the night there; but when the light from the street-lamps first fell on my face, they saw that the man they had left for dead in the woods was living still. Many an oath passed their lips as they did so, and their faces grew as pale as those of dead men.

"'I thought we had him safe enough!' growled one.

"'The gun went off,' muttered Stalker, 'and—and *something* fell—I *heard* it.'

"'Thou'st done for *the little lad* instead of his father—mark my word, that's it, Stalker!' answers a third. 'I remember the voice; and thou'lt pay it with thy life!'

"The wretched man shuddered and trembled as if he would have fallen.

"'I never meant *that*,' he gasped. 'Graham, your little lad——'

"'Thou art mad, man!' his comrades cried, and tried to shut his lips. 'Confess, and we are dead men. Think of thy wife, Stalker!'

"But he would speak.

"'I must—I must!' he whispered. 'Graham, for all I know, thy little lad lies bleeding, and maybe dead, in yon woods. I never meant *that*, God knows; *but I meant worse!*'

"I can't tell what I said then—I don't remember; I don't think I knew at the time. What I knew was just this: it was my little Robin they were talking about—some harm had come to him in the woods—I must go to him!

"I let go the man I had in charge; I cared nothing what became of him or of any of them now! I ran to the woods again as I have never run before, and there, stretched across the path, bleeding and still, lay my little lad! Well, I laid down my gun, and I took him in my arms. Then—I don't know rightly *how* I did it—but I bandaged the great, terrible wound in his forehead, and carried him home to his mother. Then it was you, friend Caleb, who told me the rest."

"Ay," says old Berry sadly, "you never knowed it afore I telled ye, Herbert, how that little, weak, girlish sort of a lad, with such a big, strong heart and courage in him, died to save his father! You see," he adds very tenderly, "it al'ays hurt him sore to call him 'little,' and now he's shown us that big people ain't al'ays so great as little 'uns. We've a deal to learn from our little Robin, Graham. I doubt if we'd 'a' done as *he* did, after all."

# DOLLY AND BIRDIE.

THE room is dark and silent,
　　The house is sad and still,
And everyone treads softly,
　　For Dolly's very ill!

Poor darling little Dolly!
　　How pale her sweet face grew!
Her eyes are large and listless,
　　That were so bright and blue.

And Dolly's head fell aching
　　When Birdie's song was sung;
So outside Dolly's window
　　His little cage is hung.

Her song once rivalled Birdie's—
So true and full of bliss!
But now her lips scarce tremble
To welcome mother's kiss.

Poor, darling little Dolly!—
But Birdie does not know
Why Dolly cannot feed him;
And he does miss her so!

And so he sings the louder
Outside her window-frame,
And tries his best to whistle
Sweet Dolly's little name.

But no one thinks of Birdie:
O'er Dolly's cot they bend,
And soothe, and tend, and love her,
Who was his little friend.

And so the hours pass slowly,
And slowly, slowly by,
With Birdie's cheery carols
And Dolly's plaintive cry.

## Dolly and Birdie.

So very faint is Birdie,
   Yet cannot find a crumb!
His seed-tin is quite empty—
   Why does not Dolly come?

Ah, happy little Dolly!
   The angels came, you know,
To take her to that country
   Where Birdie cannot go.

But while her friends weep softly,
   And call her by her name,
The Birdie still sings bravely
   Outside her window-frame.

When evening shadows lengthen,
   And Dolly's soul has fled,
With one last trill of gladness
   The Birdie too lies dead!

# A QUIET LITTLE HEROINE.

## CHAPTER I.

### HEROES.

MINNIE and Teddy Williams are twins. Their lives count eight years apiece, and sixteen put together. Minnie is a dark-haired, dark-eyed twin, and Teddy is a flaxen-haired, blue-eyed one. Both are nice, bright, lovable children; but little Minnie is quite my favourite, and I will tell you why.

Minnie is very unselfish. Minnie's self goes behind everybody else, and always comes last in Minnie's thoughts. Not so with Teddy. Teddy keeps self first and foremost, and thinks of other people afterwards, if he can find time to do both.

People say, "Ah, well, Teddy is a boy!" So he is; there can be no doubt about *that*. But I never could see why boys should be allowed to be more selfish than girls. Could you?

Our Lord, we are told, "pleased not Himself;" and certainly, if anyone could please himself safely, it would be He who knew no sin! And doesn't He himself say something about "denying" ourselves, "learning of Him," and "taking up our crosses" and following Him? I think so; and certainly no one ever learnt selfishness of Our Lord, nor dragged self along with him very far on the narrow way!

Minnie Williams is trying very hard to make her little life something like that of our dear Lord. I don't mean to say that, if you saw her, you would not think her a very everyday little mortal, merry and mischievous. When we are trying very hard to be like Our Lord, it does not often make a very big show outside; but a great, deep, strong work goes on within, and changes us slowly but surely into His beautiful likeness. Minnie tries not to please herself in anything, but to please others; and that is the very best way to please God.

Teddy had a "Book of Heroes" given to him on his last birthday by Uncle Tony; that is, a book all about men and women, and even children, who did very brave things, for which they often got a great deal of praise and glory.

Teddy thinks it would be a very grand thing to be a hero. He means to be one some day, he tells Minnie. And Minnie says she will be the very first to be proud of her hero-brother. She has no doubt but that he will be a hero some day.

As for herself, Minnie likes the stories about the heroes very much, and as she reads them aloud to Teddy, who is not fond of reading for himself, her heart beats fast; but she doesn't feel as if she would ever be able to do anything at all brave, or for which people could praise her. She just tries to live for God in her simple, daily life, giving up her own will and her own way to that of others.

The twin's father is a Lincolnshire farmer.

The farmhouse is a dear old-fashioned building, very low, with tiny latticed windows, and very long and rambling. Part of it has not been lived in for a great many years, and is going to decay as fast as it can. There the beams of the roof have fallen through, the walls have given way, and the kind grass and lichens have done their best to hide its ugliness and nakedness with green and orange patches. The children are not allowed to play in the ruins, nor even very near, for stone and brickwork are continually falling, and they might be crushed. So the owls and the bats have it all to themselves, and a fine noise they make there at night. Some silly people talked of ghosts and shivered, but we know better! Ghosts are not likely to spend their time in old ruins, crying 'To-whit! to-whoo!' and squeaking, are they?

In fine weather, Minnie and Teddy find

plenty to amuse them about the dear old farmstead, feeding the animals, playing in the lofts; or away in the green fields and shady woods. On wet days, as a tremendous treat, they are allowed to romp in the barns, and to play hide-and-seek over the house. As you may imagine, the house is just the very best place in the world for hide-and-seek. There are so many long, dark, winding passages, so many rooms, besides chinks, crannies, and corners, into which the two children manage to squeeze themselves turn by turn, making the old walls ring and echo again with their merry laughter, almost as if they meant to split their old sides.

' Bless their happy little hearts! It does one good to hear them!" says Farmer Williams, as he comes in from his work about the farm to rest a while.

To-day, warm summer day though it is, rain is pouring down from a bundle of black clouds, and the sun is shining through it as it falls, painting it lovely rain-bow colours. And the hot, thirsty earth drinks it in, and scents the air with a warm, delicious scent like that of a hot-house.

It is quite clear that Minnie and Teddy must stay in-doors to-day. So, after lessons are learnt and said, Teddy proposes to his twin a grand game at hide-and-seek.

Minnie is very busy making a pair of mittens for old Molly Brown, the washerwoman, and she is anxious to get them finished, so that she may give them to old Molly, and hear her say how warm they will keep her rheumatic fingers through the winter.

Minnie would far rather stay and knit quietly, but then winter is still a long way off, so Molly will not need the mittens yet. And Teddy *does* so want a game of hide-and-seek now! Self says "Stay!" but Minnie's good angel whispers, "Even Christ pleased not Himself." Down go the dear mittens without a sigh, and Minnie runs off to play with her twin.

"Minnie," says Teddy gleefully, "I've actually been clever enough to invent a new sort of game of hide-and-seek. We will play it to-day, and I will show you how."

"A new game, Teddy? How nice! What is it?" asks Minnie eagerly.

"Well, listen! When we went to see old Molly yesterday, while you were picking up those stupid clothes-pegs for her in the orchard, she told me a most beautiful story. Minnie, just fancy! There was once a *real live hero* living in our very own house, Minnie! A soldier hero, who fought no end of battles in countries far away, and then came here with his beautiful wife. The house was ever so much bigger then—a Hall, they called it."

"Oh, Teddy! Molly tells about such a lot of things that nobody else believes in," interrupts his twin.

"Yes, but this was *quite* true. The hero's name was Sir Godwin Firth, Molly said. Such a grand name, Minnie! You see, when I'm a hero, I can't ever be half so grand, because I can't have such a grand-sounding name. Father certainly ought to have called me something better."

"Oh, Teddy! when you've got a saint's

name!" remonstrated Minnie, "and that's ever so much better than a hero's, I'm sure!"

"Well, St. Edward *was* a king, I suppose," Teddy grunts. "But then what's the use of only being a boy? It doesn't make me king, if I have the name of a king. And I don't even get the good of my name, for I'm always called 'Teddy.' I don't suppose St. Edward ever got called Teddy! It's such a baby name."

"I think Teddy's just the beautifullest name there is!" says Minnie quickly.

"Just because you like *me*, I suppose?" grunts Teddy. "Well, Minnie—old Molly says she can just remember that time when Sir Godwin Firth lived here. It was when she was quite a little girl, and her mother was dairy-woman at the Hall. She remembers the Hall, too. It was ever so grand, with great beautiful avenues of trees leading up to it, and a park, and deer, and such a lot of wonderful things. The beautiful wife died when Sir Godwin was an old man, and he buried her under the chestnut-tree in the

Holme Field, and cried very much for her. But after a while, Molly said, he began to forget about her, and to care for something else instead—that was money."

"What a horrid man, Teddy! I *don't* think he was a hero!" exclaims Minnie.

"Molly called him a miser," Teddy goes on. "He sent away all the servants, and lived quite by himself in the old Hall. It began to fall to pieces, but he never had it mended. Nobody ever saw him. They said he used to count over his money at night, and to get richer and richer, and richer and richer and richer, every day."

"And then?" questions Minnie, seeing no end to this exaggerated version of the miser's supposed wealth.

"Then at last one day he was found dead just outside his own door, and they took him away and buried him by the side of his beautiful wife. There was nobody left to cry for him, or to be sorry when he was gone."

"Poor man—poor miser!" says Minnie sadly.

"People went seeking through the house for his money," says Teddy, "but they never found it. And then they said the house was haunted, so nobody lived here for a long time. And Molly told me that old Sir Godwin's ghost comes back every night, and counts over twenty bags full of gold in the old tumble-down part of the house. And, Minnie, Molly says there's an old, old doorway hidden in the wall somewhere here that leads right down to the treasure-room where he counts. And it's said that, if ever anyone catches him counting, he'll be forced to leave all his bags of gold behind him, and go away for ever. So now, Minnie, I'll tell you what we're going to do. I'm going to be a hero, and find the doorway, and go in, and get the gold to make me and father rich, and never be afraid of the ghosts. You must come and look too; but if you find the door first, don't open it, because *I* want to be the hero."

"Teddy," says Minnie, "I've heard that story before. It's a very silly one. Father doesn't believe it, and mother doesn't. If there ever was a Sir Godwin, what would be the use of his coming to count over his money every night, when once would do?"

"It's the sort of thing ghosts always do," says Teddy, with dignity. "Molly *says* he did it; and she's likely to know all about him, as she saw him. Father and mother don't believe in ghosts, but it's because they haven't ever seen one. Come along, Minnie! and I shall soon be a hero, like old Sir Godwin!"

"I don't think he could have been a real true hero," says Minnie, slowly following her twin, but determined not to assist in the search, "or he'd have loved his wife more and his money less. And he'd have tried to do more good with his gold than just counting it."

"I wonder how long people are expected to love their wives!" says Teddy thoughtfully. "Mayn't they give up when they are dead and no good? I don't think I shall love my wife much when she's dead!"

"Oh, Teddy, don't say such things!"

"Why?" responds Teddy, as he hurries on

in the direction of the ruins. "Come along, Minnie! You're so slow."

"We mustn't go into that part of the house, even if we do find the door that Molly talks about," says Minnie decidedly. "Mother says not, you know, Teddy!"

"Mother won't mind if I come back a rich man and a hero, with a lot of money to buy everything I want for myself, and a new silk dress for her with velvet trimming, and a fine Sunday coat for father, Minnie! She won't know how to thank me right enough!" and Teddy's eyes shine as these grand dreams of his future glory and magnificence run riot in his little head.

Minnie is no whit less anxious than himself that he should be a hero; but there is a firm resolve in her mind that she will keep her twin from disobedience if possible, even at the cost of his heroism.

"Molly said, for sure and certain, that the door was somewhere at the end of this long passage, and leading out of one of these lumber-rooms," pants forth Teddy, after a long and unsuccessful search.

"I don't believe Molly knows," says faithless Minnie.

"You are a goose, Minnie!" exclaims Teddy very ungraciously. "I don't believe you really want me to be a hero."

"Oh yes, indeed—indeed I do, dear Teddy," cries Minnie, throwing her two arms lovingly round the neck of her twin. "When you're a hero I shall be ever so glad. I suppose the Queen will send for you to live near her in London then, and father and mother'll come too. Only, isn't there any other way of being a hero, Teddy?"

"Not for me," says Teddy grandly. "But I don't give up this door yet, Minnie. Heroes always have a great lot of patience. You and I will have another hunt for it to-morrow."

## CHAPTER II.

#### THE GREATEST HERO OF ALL.

UNCLE TONY has come to stay at the farm for a few days, much to Minnie and Teddy's delight. Uncle Tony is a capital hand at everything, from telling a first-rate story (all the better because it is always true) to having a famous game of hide-and-seek. Though he is so big and tall—a giant by the side of Teddy—he always manages to squeeze himself into the most out-of-the-way places, and is harder to find than anybody else.

Besides all this, he is really a bit of a hero himself. Teddy's father told him the story, and when he heard it, Uncle Tony won Teddy's heart at once. This is how Uncle Tony became a hero:

Three little school-children were playing truant one day, sliding on a large pond. They were going along so swiftly and merrily over the smooth ice, and the sound of their voices came ringing through the air. Uncle Tony heard them, and stopped to watch them. But suddenly the ice split and broke with a terrible crash in the middle of the pond. The merry voices changed to wild screaming, and the poor little girl, who had been the boldest of the three in venturing on the ice in the centre of the pond, fell through into the ice-cold water. A moment later, and she would be drowned. For that moment Uncle Tony did not wait. He knew what ought to be done, and he did it. He laid himself down on the cracking ice, close to the hole through which the child had fallen. It was a dreadfully dangerous thing to do. Uncle Tony could not swim, and any instant the ice might split up under his weight, and let him down into the deep, dark water. When the little child rose to the surface, Uncle Tony made a dash at her frock, and managed to get hold of it. The poor little girl's clothes were soaked and heavy with water; she was quite unconscious, and could do nothing to help herself.

The other children had run away crying to tell their parents what had happened. No one was in sight or hearing of the pond. Uncle Tony raised the child out of the water, and laid her safely on the firm ice. Then all at once everything gave way beneath him, there was a horrid crash, and the waters closed over Uncle Tony's head. The little girl still lay on the ice—he had saved her life!

Just in time, one of the children's parents came down to the pond and rescued brave Uncle Tony. You may imagine how people thanked him for having saved the little girl from such a terrible death; how they praised him, and called him a hero. The strange part about it was that Uncle Tony never seemed to think he had done anything at all wonderful, or worth being made such a fuss about! He was glad the little girl was safe.

"*You* ought to know what heroes are, uncle!" says Teddy one day, sitting down tailor-wise before Uncle Tony, while little Minnie nestles into his arms. "Who do you think was the greatest hero that ever lived— *the very greatest?*"

"One Who chose to be poor and lowly, and to be set at nought and ill-treated by men— Who pleased not Himself."

Minnie looks up brightly into her uncle's face, and smiles.

"Who suffered cruelly, and at last died a shameful, painful death to save His enemies. To my thinking, He is the very greatest Hero Who ever has lived, or ever will live, Teddy boy!"

"You mean Our Lord, don't you, uncle?" says Teddy, a little disappointed by his uncle's reply to his question. "But then we can never be heroes like Our Lord, can we, uncle?"

"And why not, Teddy?"

"Oh, I mean we can never die, or be poor, or have pain, as He did. For one thing, I don't believe I've got any enemies—I really don't!"

"Then I'm extremely sorry to hear it," says Uncle Tony gravely.

"Oh, uncle," puts in Minnie, "you don't

mean to say that we are to have enemies, do you? I thought we ought to love all our enemies till they turn into friends."

Uncle Tony stoops down and kisses Minnie's little upturned face very lovingly.

"Quite right, Minnie," he says; "I did not mean that. The enemies that we must hate— yes, and strive against to our lives' end—are our bad feelings. Those are our enemies to the death. Do you know, Teddy boy, it *has* sometimes just occurred to me that you treat your enemy Selfishness a little too much as if he were your friend. Don't you think so?"

Teddy doesn't answer. His head is squeezed tightly between his knees, and he is watching a spider that is doing its best to weave its web from Uncle Tony's chair to the floor.

"Then about the rest," goes on Uncle Tony, "I don't believe there ever can be a true hero unless he is more or less like the Grand Hero, Our Lord Jesus Christ. We may not be called to make ourselves very poor, or to die for others, as you say; but still we *are* called *to live* for them, and so to be like Our Lord in not pleasing ourselves. Try it, Teddy, and see if it is not the greatest heroism of all. To be sure, it may not bring you great praise from men; but what a poor, mean thing their honour and glory is, at the best! Christ's heroes and heroines shall be confessed and honoured before God and the holy angels one day."

"I will try to be one of His heroines, uncle," whispers little Minnie softly. "I do try every day, uncle."

"That's right, my Minnie," says Uncle Tony.

"Uncle," puts in Teddy, who finds the conversation getting far too grave for his liking, "that spider's gone into your pocket this minute—I saw it!"

"All right, Teddy boy!" and Uncle Tony flaps out his handkerchief and the spider on to the floor. "He is a hero, too, in his way," says Uncle Tony; "he does great things with very little! But, Teddy, I want you to begin to think about my plan for becoming one of the true heroes—won't you?"

"Some day," drawls Teddy awkwardly; and then he runs away to play with baby Ruth, the little two-year-old cousin who has come with Uncle Tony to pay them a visit.

## CHAPTER III.

### OUR LITTLE HEROINE.

It is early morning.

The sun is not awake yet. The sky looks grey. Stars shine; and down below the earth is dim and misty.

Most people are still asleep. The old farmhouse is silent, and all eyes quietly closed in it except two.

Little Minnie is awake.

She has slipped out of bed, drawn aside the curtains from the window, and is peeping out. It is so quiet and peaceful out there. Minnie likes watching it. The long, grey meadows stretch far away to the line of the horizon on the left. On the right a wing of the house stands out a good way; and beyond it are the orchards and the dark thick wood.

And the golden stars look down upon it all, like beautiful angels keeping watch.

"I wonder if Teddy would like a peep too?" thinks Minnie.

But Teddy's flaxen curls are all that can be seen of him at present, and the only sound from his crib is a contented snore now and then.

Minnie does not like to wake him. She will just take one more look herself, and then go back to bed again.

This time Minnie notices that there is a light shining brightly in the right wing of the house. That is where little Ruth sleeps, with Norah, the servant.

Uncle Tony has been away from home with father for a few days. They must have come back early this morning, thinks Minnie.

Did mother go down to unlock the door for them, or how did they get in? Perhaps father had a latch-key with him, and so they let themselves in!

What is the light burning there for now? It will soon be quite light everywhere. A few long red streaks in the sky down near the horizon show that the sun means to be up very soon.

As Minnie stands before the window, watching the light, and wondering what it can mean, it suddenly grows brighter and larger. A great jet of flame shines out at a window, and reflects itself brightly upon the whole length of the wall. A rush of thick smoke eddies through the closed window-frames. Minnie smells the strong, suffocating smell as it penetrates even to where she is standing. Then, all at once, the terrible truth flashes across her—the house is on fire!

"Fire! Fire!" calls a little voice. "Fire! Fire!"

Teddy awakes startled, and follows his twin with quick, frightened steps into mother's room, which is some way off. But mother has heard the cry of fire, and even begun to smell the smoke. When the children reach her, she is trying to hurry on some of her clothes, to go and see what is the matter.

"Run to Norah, Minnie dear," she says. "Tell her to dress Ruth as quickly as possible, and carry her to Molly Brown's cottage for safety."

Minnie obeys at once; and when she comes back, mother bids both children dress, and follow her to rouse the labourers.

Very soon a crowd of men are gathered round the old house, pouring pailful after pailful of water upon the part where the flames have broken out, if possible to keep them in check until the engines, which have been sent for, arrive.

No one has any idea of how the fire happened, and there is no time now to inquire about it. Everyone is busy doing his best to put out the flames. Even little Teddy and Minnie are of use in carrying empty pails to the pump to be filled.

The worst of it is that father and Uncle Tony are still away, and no one quite knows where to find them; and the fire is spreading fast, in spite of all they can do.

"Poor old house!" say the men; "it'll be almost a miracle if it don't get burnt down to the ground. Them old beams are as good as touchwood for taking fire!"

It is a grand sight, very—though such a terrible one. Those great red, roaring flames have burned away the window-frames to charcoal, and lick the walls with eager tongues outside, flaring away into the dense mass of smoke for many yards away. It is well that the stackyard lies on the other side of the house, and that the wind is not that way, or the ricks would stand but a poor chance against that great mass of flame.

Mrs. Williams has given orders that everything moveable is to be carried from the house to the barn for safety. And it is well that she has done so, for by the time all the more valuable articles have gone, the fire is bursting out in every direction, and the dust and noise of walls beginning to fall mingle with the roar of the flames and the blinding rush of smoke.

The firemen are just thinking that they must leave the old house to its fate, and lead away their engines to protect the barns, which are really in danger now, when there is the sound of horses' hoofs, and Farmer Williams with Uncle Tony ride up to the crowd before the house in hot haste, their horses steaming and panting. They saw the burning house when they were some miles away, and have ridden as fast as their horses could carry them.

Farmer Williams at once hurries off to the barns with the engines, and Uncle Tony anxiously asks Mrs. Williams where is his child, his little Ruth?

"I gave Norah orders to take her to Molly Brown's cottage, as soon as we discovered the fire," she answers. "You will find her there, Tony. I only hope the poor dear child was not much frightened. I have not had time to see about her."

Uncle Tony hurries away to Molly's cottage, but in a few moments he comes back pale and breathless.

"Ruth is not there!" he gasps. "Molly tells me she has seen nothing of her."

"You don't say so, Tony!" cries Mrs. Williams, with a very troubled face. "Then where can Norah have taken her?"

"The girl is there, in violent hysterics," answers Uncle Tony. "But where, oh! where is my little Ruthie?"

"I do not know; I cannot tell," falters Mrs. Williams. "Surely she *cannot* have been left in the house? Oh, Tony!"

As she speaks, above the noise of the flames, and the crash of falling walls and timbers, there comes a terrible cry from a chamber overhead. They both hear it clearly.

"It is Ruth," their hearts say, though neither of them speak.

Uncle Tony hastens away to see if he can force his way up the burning stairs to his child's room.

In vain! The stairs are a mass of flame and blinding, stifling smoke, and he turns back baffled. The next thing is to raise a long ladder to the window. This is soon done, and the frantic father mounts it to save his child.

It is very unsafe, for the room below is all giving way, but Uncle Tony never thinks of the danger. All his thought is for his child—his little Ruth!

But, alas! when the window is opened, it is too narrow. He cannot force his way through to her.

"Ruth," he calls; "come to the window! Come quick!"

The little child sits up in bed, still screaming with terror at the smoke and flame, but she does not obey him.

"Ruthie! Ruthie! Do you hear me?" calls her father again and again. The child neither moves nor speaks.

Only the crackling of the flames grows louder and nearer.

Uncle Tony comes down the ladder again in despair.

"I cannot reach her," he says. "The window is too small—too narrow! Oh, is there anyone who can and will save my darling child!"

"Uncle Tony, I will go," says a small voice; and Minnie comes forward, pale, but very resolute.

"Minnie, my own child, I cannot let you go!" cries her mother, holding her back.

"I am not afraid, mother," Minnie says bravely. "If I do not go, little Ruth will be burnt to death. Oh, let me go, mother!"

"Tony," cries the poor mother piteously, "you will see that she returns safely, won't you? It would break my heart if aught should happen to her."

"God helping me, I will be answerable for her," replies Uncle Tony very solemnly. And when he turns round once more, he sees Minnie already climbing the ladder. He mounts it after her.

"Hold the ladder firm as a rock for your lives, lads!" he calls to the men below. Then he opens the window, and little Minnie manages to squeeze herself through.

The smoke almost blinds her as she gropes her way to the crib in the far corner of the room, where lies little Ruth, quite stupefied now with smoke and fear.

The brave little girl takes her in her arms, and carries her to Uncle Tony, who is waiting to receive his child at the open window.

Another short moment, and she is safe on the ground below. Uncle Tony begins to mount the ladder once more for Minnie, when there is a sudden crash, the ladder gives way, and falls heavily to the ground. The whole building for a moment totters and almost heaves over. The roof slides down with clouds of timber, brick, and mortar. When all is clear again, little Minnie has disappeared.

The poor anxious mother watching, when she sees her little child no more, gives one wild cry, and falls fainting. She is carried away to old Molly's cottage, and meanwhile Uncle Tony, with a face full of anguish and despair, is trying his utmost to raise a ladder against the broken house once more—all in vain!

And Minnie, brave, unselfish Minnie! our true-hearted little heroine! has she perished in the raging flames from which she has so nobly saved her baby-cousin? or does she lie buried in the ruins of the house?

You shall hear.

## CHAPTER IV.

#### THE SECRET DOOR.

BRUISED and stunned, Minnie lies for a while near where once the window stood. It is gone now, and in its place lie heaped masses of broken brick-work, through whose chinks light steals faintly into the room.

As soon as the stunned feeling has passed off, Minnie gets up from the floor and looks about her.

A terrible fear seizes the poor child when she sees all that has happened. They will never be able to save her by the ladder now, and those cruel flames are rushing on from within, eager to burn her to death.

Oh, such an earnest prayer goes up to heaven from little Minnie's heart that God will be with her in her danger and loneliness, and find some way to save her yet!

And when she has prayed it, she feels comforted.

The angel was with the three children in the very midst of the cruel flames, and Minnie feels sure that God's good angels are very near her now.

But there is no time to be lost. The smoke will stifle her here if she stays much longer. So the poor child gropes her way over brick, beam, and fallen furniture out of the room as best she may, and down the long passage to the stairs.

Here, too, all chance of escape is cut off.

The stairs are burnt away to charred fragments—they are only a black mass in the midst of roaring flames coming always nearer —nearer!

Minnie turns away, and dashes down the passage yet further.

"The fire will reach the ruins last, anyway," she thinks; "perhaps, if I can stay long enough at that end of the house, they may have time to find out where I am, and to save me still. It won't be disobedience to go there, for I know mother wouldn't tell me to stay and be burnt, if she only knew!"

Poor little burnt feet they are, that limp so quickly over those heated boards! Poor little scorched face, that smarts so painfully, with the pretty dark curls, all spoilt and singed, hanging round it!

But Minnie never thinks of her face, or of her feet. On—on she hurries, through the smoke, and over the rubbish-heaps lying in her way—on towards that part of the house where, only a few days ago, Teddy told her he would find the secret door, get possession of Sir Godwin Firth's treasures, and be a real hero.

That time seems strangely long ago now to poor little Minnie as she thinks of it. It feels as if years even might have flown away since then.

On, on, still on, go those weary little feet, leaving the smoke, fire, and noise alike behind them.

She stops at last, not because she has reached the end of her travels and is safe, but that just before her is a broken doorway which she has never seen before. Beyond it, all is quite dark. The door itself has fallen down, and lies across the way. It is an old oaken door, in shape more like a shutter than a door. This must surely be one way into the ruins, thinks Minnie. *Can* it be the very door of which old Molly told Teddy a few days ago?

If so, she may perhaps find a way out of her troubles by it. But again Minnie's timid little heart beats fast, for if the door is truly there, may not old Molly be right also in her tales about Sir Godwin Firth?

Minnie has no mind to go and meet the wretched old miser counting his gold!

She waits and thinks a little before venturing into the darkness, though she feels sure that, sooner or later, it must lead her out of reach of that dreadful fire coming on so fast behind her.

"Mother says," thinks Minnie, "ghosts don't come in that sort of way to frighten people. If they're wicked ghosts, I suppose they'll be kept shut up somewhere, and never allowed to come out. If they're good ghosts, then they're sure to be with God, and they won't ever want to come. Mother would say I'm wrong to be afraid!"

So, gathering up all her courage, and trusting to her good Angel Guardian, Minnie steps over the door, and takes a first step into the darkness beyond, groping her way along by the damp, dust-covered walls.

After a time the place begins to grow lighter. The kind roof has fallen through in parts, and let daylight in. Just before her Minnie sees a narrow stone staircase, winding away down into the darkness. Down she must go; there is nothing else for it.

The stairs wind round and round, until Minnie is tired and dizzy; then they suddenly stop, and she finds herself in a large, low room, just dimly lighted by a small iron grating, deeply set in the wall, and half choked with the dust of years.

So far, at least, she has seen nothing of Sir Godwin, and poor Minnie begins to feel less frightened.

But now for the way out. Where can it be? Surely this large low room cannot be the very end of everywhere?

After a long hunt, Minnie finds an old, old door, heavily barred and clamped with iron. The rusty padlock still hangs to it, as it may have hung for eighty years or more. This must be the way out, for there are no signs of any other.

Minnie tries to pull the heavy bolts aside with her tiny fingers, and to undo the great padlock; but, of course, her little strength is of no avail. They will not even tremble, much less move, and at last she gives it up as useless.

"I might just as well have stayed where I was!" thinks the poor child sadly. Then, as she listens, she feels glad that she has not; for even here the roar and smell of the fire are following her.

"They will never hear me if I call, or find out where I am, until perhaps I'm dead and starved—and perhaps not even then!" says poor Minnie, crying bitter tears at the thought. "I shall never see Teddy when he's a hero, or be able to tell him how glad I am! I shall never see father and mother any more—never again! I shall be left here all alone in the dark, dark, dark—till I die! Oh, it is dreadful—dreadful!"

Then a little voice whispers to Minnie's heart that there is still one hope for her.

Minnie's eyes fall upon the small iron grating through which the light creeps. Once up there, she may be able to call for help to those outside, and let them know where she is.

Wearily the poor child clambers up the uneven wall, and seats herself upon the stone ledge below the grating. She can look out now, and a dreary prospect it is! Only the dark walls of the ruined house all round and far above her, moss and weed-grown!

"Father! father!" calls the child again and again, and her voice echoes through the dreary chamber; but never an answer comes "Mother! Uncle Tony!"

Such a long, long time, and still no one comes or seems to hear. Poor little lonely Minnie! her voice is too weak now to call any longer; she is faint with hunger, and full of pain all over from the cuts, burns, and bruises which cover her poor little body. All the long day she has had nothing to eat, and now it must be drawing near even.

Minnie leans her tired head against the window, and, hard and comfortless as her resting-place is, she soon forgets hunger and pain in sleep.

Such a strange dream she has as she lies there, with her small dark head pressed against the grating, like a prisoner of the olden days, and perhaps as forlorn and hopeless as any of them were!

Old Sir Godwin rises up before Minnie in

her dream, dressed as a knight of old, with a steel helmet, gorgeous cloak, and armour shining beneath it, and twenty great bags chinking in his hands.

She sees him open the bags one by one, and out on to the floor from each flows a glittering golden stream of coins, which he counts over with the point of his sword.

Minnie even sees the eager, greedy glare of his eyes as he fixes them upon his work and counts on, on, on, always on, and over and over again, as if he would never be tired.

Then Teddy comes in, and Minnie holds out her arms to him, and begs him to show her the way out of this horrible place. But Teddy will not look at her; he is going to be a hero, and he goes up to Sir Godwin, and tries to seize one of the money-bags.

Minnie bursts out crying at Teddy's unkindness, and then Sir Godwin Firth and her dream vanish together, and she awakes, rubbing her tearful eyes with her dusty 'hands. The morning light is shining brightly in through the grating.

Minnie does not remember where she is or what has happened for some time. Then it all comes back to her. She raises herself up once more, and begins to call with all her might:

"Uncle Tony! Uncle Tony!"

But her voice is very weak—there is scarcely an echo to it this morning; and all the hopeless thoughts of yesterday crowd back to the poor little maiden in her prison.

"They cannot hear, and they will not come! I shall never see any of them again—never again! Hark! what is that noise?"

A dull, grating sound falls upon Minnie's ear—very far distant, but as if coming nearer. In an instant Minnie's last night's dream flashes into her mind. This must surely be Sir Godwin coming to count his gold!

He is coming, and she will have to face him. Minnie grows quite pale and white with the thought. Her poor little limbs tremble with fear as she peers anxiously round and round the gloomy chamber.

But time goes on, and Sir Godwin never

makes his appearance, though the noise does not stop. Nearer and nearer it comes. Then a voice:

"Minnie, Minnie! Where are you, Minnie?"

Surely it is Uncle Tony's voice! Minnie tries to answer joyfully:

"Here, Uncle Tony—here!"

But her voice is only a whisper that nobody could possibly hear.

"He is coming—Uncle Tony is coming!" thinks the little maiden, as she waits anxiously.

But the noise stops.

A new fear comes to torment poor Minnie.

"Uncle Tony could not hear me call. He thinks I am not here, and is gone away!"

Soon the noise begins again—this time quite close at hand. The old iron door rattles violently. Then Minnie hears men at work with picks and hammers to burst it open. There are the gruff voices of some of her father's labourers, and Uncle Tony is cheering them on.

The old door shivers for an instant, then comes down with a tremendous crash, and

Uncle Tony has his dear little niece in his arms.

"You are come at last," Minnie says, very faintly; "and I have been calling for you, oh, so long, Uncle Tony!"

"I never heard you, Minnie darling," says Uncle Tony, as he carries her in his strong arms out of the dark chamber and through the ruins by a way she has never been before. "The fire is out now. And ever since we lost you, father and I have been searching everywhere, and almost giving up all hope of finding you. But this morning old Molly reminded me of the old door between the house and the ruins, and by this means, thank God, we have our Minnie safe once more!"

Minnie doesn't say another word until they reach old Molly's cottage. Now that the terrible fear of never being found again is gone, she is content to rest quietly in her uncle's arms, and to feel very weak, but very glad.

At the cottage-door father and mother both meet her, and laugh and cry over her by turns, which Minnie thinks very funny indeed.

Teddy looks at his twin from a respectful distance, with a kind of solemn awe on his face. For Minnie has spent a whole night in that mysterious ruined chamber of which he has only dreamed.

Little Ruth toddles up to Minnie, lisping her name in baby-fashion, and kisses her everywhere—over face, frock, and hands. Uncle Tony has managed to make the little girl understand in some way or other that, but for Minnie, she might have been burnt to death in that dreadful fire; and Ruth feels very grateful to Minnie in her baby way.

Of course they give poor Minnie something to eat the first thing, but she has been hungry so long that she can only swallow a little of the food they bring her, whereat Teddy is much amazed.

Fancy having had nothing to eat all yesterday, and then not being ready for your breakfast to-day!

Teddy would like to ask Minnie some questions as to whether she has seen or heard anything of old Sir Godwin down in those wonderful ruins; but no sooner does he open his mouth than Uncle Tony puts up a very solemn finger that means " silence," and Teddy is obliged to swallow his curiosity for a little while.

"Where is Norah?" Minnie asks presently.

" Norah was sent home this morning," says mother. "But for Norah's disobedience we should never have had all this trouble about our darling Minnie."

" Poor Norah! I remember now," says Minnie. "She never took Ruthie to old Molly's, as I told her to, and so——"

" And so," says Uncle Tony, taking up Minnie's words, and finishing them for her in his own way, "our little Minnie—brave, unselfish little Minnie!—put herself into danger to save Ruthie. And Uncle Tony will never be able to hold enough gratitude in his heart to thank her properly!"

" What nonsense, Uncle Tony!" protests Minnie. "Of course——" and then she does not know what to say next.

Just at that moment a labourer comes to

call Mr. Williams away. There is great excitement going on at the ruins about something or other.

Then Uncle Tony goes over to Mrs. Williams and says, "Sister, Burnham House will hold your whole tribe until your own place can be rebuilt. Won't you come and stay with us for a while? I can't make up my mind to part with your dear little Minnie just yet."

And Mrs. Williams gladly says yes, if her husband will agree to the plan.

Presently the farmer joins them again.

"Tony," he says, "will you come to the ruins for a moment. The men have made a grand find there. It seems that old Molly's stories of the miserly Sir Godwin have really some foundation after all, for they have found some hundreds of old gold sovereigns secreted in the wall of that old chamber—more than enough to rebuild the house, if I can fairly claim the money."

"No one will dispute your right to what is found on your own property," answers Uncle Tony, "unless it is the old miser himself, who is supposed to appear nightly to count it over!"

"It is so odd that it should have lain there year after year, without anyone finding it!" says Mr. Williams.

"It has lain hidden, like many other good things," says Uncle Tony, with a smile. "Who would have guessed, for instance, that your little eight-year-old Minnie had in her the making of a heroine?"

When they reach the ruins, the sight of the gold dazzles and astonishes Uncle Tony. If Minnie could see it, she would think that her dream of last night had really come true.

"Well, whatever the old miser may have done in his life-time," says Uncle Tony, "he is certainly doing good years and years after his death, in rebuilding your house, Williams! There's nothing like burning down your house if you want to find treasure, evidently. I fancy I shall try it! But, seriously, Williams, until your house is set right by Sir Godwin and his gold, won't you take up your abode, all of you, at Burnham House? We shall be delighted to welcome you—shan't we, my Ruthie?"

And Mr. Williams promises that they will do so, much to Minnie's joy.

"We can put up Master Teddy in the pig-stye, I suppose, if there's no room anywhere else," says Uncle Tony, in his droll way.

Teddy gives a grunt, which reminds one very much of the despised creatures who dwell in the said styes.

"I shall never, never, never be able to be a hero now, as I thought I should!" the young man remarks, with a sigh, shortly after. "The secret door has been opened, and Sir Godwin's money has been found!"

"Minnie—our quiet little brown mouse, Minnie—is the heroine!" says Uncle Tony, with such a loving, grateful look at his little niece that she turns quite shy, and blushes like a red rose.

"Uncle," she stammers, "don't, please! I only——"

"Only learnt those five little words by heart, and lived up to them," says Uncle Tony, again taking up her sentence in his own way: "'Even Christ pleased not Himself.'

And those words taught little Minnie that not to discover secret doors and golden coin, not to be great in the sight of men, but to put away self, is the truest heroism of all. And Minnie has followed that rule until she has become one of the Great Hero's own children—His little Heroine.

# SIX LITTLE SISTERS.

SIX little sisters, so merry and gay—
    Hair of all colours, save snowy or grey;—
    Brownie and golden, golden and brown;
Twisted and plaited, and hanging down.
Cheeks pale or rosy, or colour of peach;
Lips like ripe cherries have all, and have each;
Eyes brown as berries, coal-black, or as blue
As the sky—a sure sign that their owner is true!

Six little sisters to stand on the floor;
Six little sisters to file through the door;
Six little sisters to laugh or to cry;
Six little sisters to smile or to sigh;

Six little sisters to dance in the light;
Six little sisters to sleep through the night
Six little sisters, as merry as crickets—
To tear their white frocks in the thorns and the thickets.

Six little sisters—a class without more—
Trying to add to the length of their lore;
Six little sisters for multiplication;
Six little sisters to do their dictation.
Six little sisters for A, B, and C;
Six little sisters for sewing at three.
In summing, be sure they are ne'er in a fix,
For they *always* remember that six ones are six!

Six little sisters, *so* precious and dear!
Close to perfection (won't reach it, I fear!);
Six little sisters, all careless of care,
Six little sisters, and not *one* to spare!
Six little maidens—*much* better than boys!—
Famed for their powers of making a noise.
Six little sisters their "pieces" to strum;
Six little sisters to sit on a thumb!

Six *sweet* little sisters; they come to you now
With a smile and a frown, and a speech and a
  bow.
Six *dear* little sisters—as good as red gold,
Who yet may be better *some* day, we are told!
Six little sisters, in best bibs and tuckers,
Ribbons and frilligigs, flounces and puckers;
Six little sisters, so coaxing and gay,
To beg for a holiday once in a way!

Well, they shall have it, then! Back in dis-
  grace,
Pack all the lesson-books into their place.
Down in the kitchen teaze cook, till she bakes
For the six little sisters six giant plum-cakes.
This is their holiday—fun, falls, and knocks—
Don't shake your head, nurse, o'er rents in the
  frocks;
Never mind scratches and tanglesome curls—
They are six little sisters—and girls *will* be
  girls!

# "OLD CLO'ES."

## CHAPTER I.

### HIMSELF.

ALL day long, down one after another of London's thronging back streets and alleys, rings that melancholy voice—deep, yet shrill; mournful, yet almost comical—in its never-ending, never-changing cry of "Buy yer old clo'es—old clo'es!"

A very old man the voice belongs to. A little old man, with a bent back, and a large bag slung upon it. He has a small, dark, wrinkled face, with faded blue eyes, and cheeks each boasting one little patch of red, which, set in the nut-brown of his complexion, reminds one very much of the last russet apples left hanging on the trees in autumn. His cry might easily be taken for an advertisement of himself, to judge by the state of his clothes. His coat, once of a brilliant blue, that is to say, many years ago, is shady now, and adorned with a few brass buttons down the front, and with half a dozen shanks where the buttons themselves are wanting. His lower garment is nondescript—a clever compound of patches of various shades and shapes that seem to have been neatly mended once upon a time, but now let a little daylight in at the seams. He wears quite a stack of old chimney-pot hats, one above the other, as a sort of advertisement of his business. From under them shocks of grey hair fall, and hang in jagged fringes over the old blue coat-collar. Such is our old man in appearance—a very bundle of old clothes, and such is also his name—"Old Clo'es." Nobody ever calls him anything else. He wouldn't know who they meant if they did. He has gone by the name ever since he first took up that line of business, fifty years ago. He has almost forgotten his " Chrissen name " by now.

By-the-bye, you may as well hear what his trade is before we begin our story. Old Clo'es will buy any old garments you may have to spare, at the lowest prices, to sell them again, when they have been patched and pieced by odd bits from other garments. That materials and shades should match is no object with Old Clo'es' customers.

Old Clo'es lives in an attic in a wretched house in Scrub's Alley. There is a big hole in the ceiling, and also another to match exactly underneath it in the flooring. Old Clo'es looks upon the second hole as rather an advantage than otherwise. It allows the rain to find a short cut downstairs when it drips through the roof; and, besides that, it serves him instead of a bell when he wishes to call Lotty, the little drudge below, to attend to his wants.

Now let us follow Old Clo'es in his slow march through the streets with that same mournful cry: "Buy yer old clo'es!" He seems to be driving a pretty brisk trade this evening in the purchasing line. Many dirty newspaper parcels are handed out to him by the wretched inmates of those miserable lodgings, and many a small coin does he give in exchange, after long chaffering, from the bottom of an old leather purse that somehow manages to find a safe corner in the pocket of his ragged trousers.

Old Clo'es has nearly reached his journey's end, for he is at the entrance to Scrub's Alley, when he feels his coat-tails suddenly pulled from behind, and himself brought up short by a miserable-looking woman, who, after she has caught his attention, places herself just before him, her wan, wasted face turned towards his, and her black, piercing, hungry eyes fixed upon him.

"Mester," she says, in a trembling, imploring tone, "I see'd ye give a copper to a little hungry lass this morning, an' ye treated another to a cakie yesterday. Be ye fond o' the little lasses, mester?"

She waits there for his answer, and her eyes seem almost to search it out before he speaks.

"Missus, you're right," he says, with a little sigh, and something of a glistening comes about his eyes. "I've always a heart for the little lasses now. I'd one of my own once, ye see; but that were werry long ago. An' I'm fond o' the little 'uns for her sake—werry fond of 'em all!"

"An' I've a little lass," the woman goes on eagerly; "a pretty little lass—maybe like yourn was—hungerin' an' pinin' away afore my eyes, an' me with never a copper to get her so much as a crust! Mester, have pity on my little lass! I've sell't every scrap o' furnitur'; I've sell't every rag I could spare. Mester, ye wouldn't never let a little lass like yourn starve!"

Old Clo'es does not need to be asked twice. He draws the old purse from his pocket once more, and the woman's eagerly outstretched hands soon clasp a few of his hardly won coppers.

"God bless ye, mester!" she says earnestly.

As she turns away, Old Clo'es whispers, with a very trembling voice:

"Tell that little lass o' yourn that it's a mester as loves little 'uns as sent it her."

And then he hurries away to his home in Scrub's Alley.

## CHAPTER II.

#### A BUNDLE OF OLD CLOTHES.

It is getting late in the evening. The lamps have been lit long ago in the streets of London. Scrub's Alley, being lampless, is growing shadowy and dark. It is only here and there lit up by flickering candles in the shutterless windows.

It is late for Old Clo'es to be out, but his cry is still sounding through the streets—"Old clo'es to buy! Old clo'es!"

It has been a bad day for the old man.

## A Bundle of Old Clothes.

Cold and rain have fought together against him. The poor people who live in those streets and alleys have need of all their extra coverings to-day, and Old Clo'es' stock-in-hand has hardly grown larger since morning.

Seven o'clock sounds from a neighbouring church-tower. Old Clo'es gives it up in despair at last, and is turning homewards, when, from the darkest shade of a doorway, he is greeted by a woman's voice.

"Mester," it says, in a half-hesitating way, "you was crying out for old clo'es, wasn't you? I'll—I'll let you have this here bundle; you may have it cheap an' all."

She never stirs out of the shade of the doorway as she speaks, and all that Old Clo'es can see is the outline of a tall, thin woman, with some sort of a bundle in her arms.

He comes a few steps nearer to her.

"It's werry dark here, missus," he says; "can't you step out into the light a bit, so as I may see the things?"

"I'm—I'm lame, an' tired," falters the woman. "You may take 'em, mester, an' give me what ye please for 'em. I'm main weary carryin' of 'em about this many a day."

As she speaks, the woman holds out her bundle to him—but slowly, half holding back, as though she were loth to part with the last treasures belonging to her. Then, after what seems to be a great struggle with herself, she puts it into his arms.

"Ye may take it, mester," she says sadly. "I've held out agin this till I can hold out no longer. You're a good man, I know, and I'm nigh clemmed. Take it, and give me what ye please to buy me a morsel of bread. It's better so."

"It's a werry uncommon heavy bundle," says Old Clo'es, as the woman gives her burden into his hands.

"It's all I have in the world," whimpers the woman. "Take it, and let me go, for I'm starving!"

"I'll give you a shillin' for the lot," says Old Clo'es slowly. "I'm not in luck to-day, else maybe I might have afforded a trifle more, seein' you're so down in the world."

The leather purse gives up its shilling's-worth of coppers, and Old Clo'es trudges on his way home.

The woman watches him with keen, hawk-like eyes until he turns the corner.

"He's a kind man," she mutters to herself, brushing her hand sharply over those keen eyes of hers. "I reckon I've done my best for it. Eh! it's hard to be poor, but it's worse to starve!"

Then she leaves the doorway and speeds down the street, more like a swift-footed hare than a lame, starving woman.

Old Clo'es reaches home very weary, and rather downcast after the day's ill-luck.

He seats himself in his old arm-chair by the dying embers of the fire to rest, and sets his bundles down beside him. He pays no heed to the preparations Lotty is making for his tea, though his favourite dish of onions is on the table, and pleasant fumes from the teapot are filling the little attic.

Lotty, a pale, overgrown, big-eyed girl of thirteen or thereabouts, bustles about the room, from tiny corner-cupboard to table and back again several times. Then her task is done—for there is never much to put on Old Clo'es' table—and she comes up to the old man's chair.

Old Clo'es' head is very low on his knees. Kind-hearted Lotty feels sorry for him.

"You're quite down and tired out, mester," she says, "an' the tea 'll freshen you. Draw your chair nigh the table. Has anything been vexin' you, mester?"

Old Clo'es rouses himself, and looks up at the girl's questioning face with a sad smile.

"It's mainly the old trouble," he says sadly. "Folks say (an' maybe they're right—maybe they are), 'You ought to have forgotten an old pain like that long enough ago, mester.' It's nigh upon fifty years agone now, Lotty, but I must carry it down to my grave. She was such a *nice* little 'un, Lotty, with blue eyes and gold hair; and so angel-like, all but for want o' the wings! And she did love her father so!—*Dad* she used to call him. She was scarce five year old when she was took—

quite sudden in the night—and there's been the trouble in my heart goin' achin' on ever since. *Little Nell* we called her—never aught else. And now I never can see a little lass with blue eyes and gold hair but I think o' my own little lass as was took away, as I loved, and as loved me! There was a little 'un to-day werry like, and minded me of her till I could scarce bear it no longer. She was so hungry and pale, was the little lass; so I says to her, says I, 'Little lass, maybe you'd like a bit to eat?' And her eyes lightened up, and she put her little hand in mine ever so trustful, to go and buy a cakie. Lotty, I wish I'd my own little lass now! I'm old, and it's werry lonesome at times, you see.'

"Do you believe in them angels, and the happy place, and the bad place, an' people bein' took to one o' the two when they dies, mester?" asks Lotty eagerly. "A little brother o' mine died just a while agone, an' they said the angels took him to the bright place, where he'll never be nought but happy. Do you believe that's true, mester?"

"Well, I don't rightly know," Old Clo'es answers slowly and thoughtfully. "I've considered it many a time, and there ain't much to go upon, either ways. People don't *see* no angels goin' about. I never see'd none come for my little lass, an' I never took eyes off her till she were laid in the ground. Nor I never hear tell of that happy place i' the newspapers —neither where it be sitivated, nor nothin'; an' they do mention most things in the newspapers!"

"It 'ud be nice to think as your little Nell was in a werry pleasant, comfor'ble place— wouldn't it, mester?" says Lotty.

"Werry nice, in a way," says Old Clo'es slowly. "But I can't think *she'd* ever be werry happy wivout her farver; she'd get a-shoutin' of him ever so hard! An' then there be *two* places, Lotty—a good 'un and a bad 'un—I've heard say; an' I don't rightly know what rules they have for settlin' folks atwixt 'em, so as not to get overfull. I shouldn't like to think o' my little lass bein' i' the one, an' me in the other, an' no ways o' reachin' her, Lotty! It 'ud be worse nor not seein' her again, Lotty."

"Most things o' that sort goes by famerlies, doesn't they, mester?" suggests Lotty, by way of comfort.

"But even then there's often a deal of onfair dealin'," answers Old Clo'es sagely. "I wonder if them angels is to be reckoned on? They ain't like humans, I suppose—not bodily."

"I'd like to know as it were all good an' true," says Lotty, with a sigh. "I've heerd tell a long while ago as there was a church near here, called St. Mary's, where there's folks that knows the angels an' all about 'em well. I can't tell whether it was St. Mary herself—likely it was; but she may be dead by now."

"I've passed churches many a time o' my rounds," says Old Clo'es; "but I can't say as I've ever had the curiosity to go and see who lived in 'em. P'r'aps it's angels—leastways, I've seen very respec'able-looking folk go in at the big doors."

There is a rap of summons on the floor for Lotty at this moment, and she scuds away to answer it.

"Ay, I'd be glad to know the truth on it!" Old Clo'es mutters to himself, when Lotty is gone, as he draws his chair to the table, and bethinks himself for the first time that his tea has not been getting warmer for waiting so long.

Tea over, he draws his bags and bundles nearer to the light of the dip, puts on his spectacles, and begins to sort out and inspect what he has brought home.

The floor is soon covered with little heaps of old clothes. Each garment tells a sad tale of its own quietly, of want and misery, if not of drink and vice.

They are mostly women's clothes; old bonnets, shawls, and even threadbare scanty petticoats. Old Clo'es busies himself amongst them all for some time, reckoning up each with pencil and paper, in a manner that no one but himself could ever understand. Old Clo'es can neither read nor write now. He has forgotten the small stock of "larnin'" he once got in his youth.

At last he comes to the bundle he bought from the lame woman whom he met in the doorway. It is a bundle of a sort that Old Clo'es never meets with, except when things have come to the very worst with the poor owners :—a roll of little child's clothing, carefully wrapped one above the other, and neatly patched and mended. A poor mother must be at starvation point before she can make up her mind to sell her child's clothes; and Old Clo'es feels a half-sob rise in his throat as he unrolls the little things, which, one after another, remind him so painfully of what his own little Nell used to wear fifty years ago.

Old Clo'es has kept his heart very young and tender in the midst of his hard, rough life. Tears come into his eyes, and half blind him as he turns the things over. But, dim as his eyes are, with the last unwrapping of that bundle, Old Clo'es sees something that makes him start back in alarm and tremble all over. What can it be?

He has uncovered the little, dead face of a child—a little girl, scarcely four years of age! Long golden hair falls round her face, and a tiny, thin hand peeps out among the rags with which she is covered.

Old Clo'es' first thought is to call up Mrs. Clark, his landlady, and Lotty; but on second thoughts he decides not to do so.

Just a faint tinge of pink growing in the face of the little one has caught his eye. Old Clo'es bends over her. She is not dead yet. Her little soft hand is still warm, and breath still comes from her lips. But she seems in a very deep sleep. Old Clo'es tenderly unfastens the rags in which she is wrapped; then, kneeling on the floor, he takes her in his arms, and rocks her gently to and fro.

"Wake up, little Nell!" Old Clo'es murmurs, in the soft, cooing tones he used many years ago. His poor head is in a sad whirl, and he forgets that this child cannot be his lost little Nell.

"Wake up, little Nell! It's your own Dad as is here!"

But he speaks in vain. Those tiny hands hang limply over his arms; the child never opens her eyes.

Old Clo'es still kneels there, forgetting how cramped and stiff his knees are becoming. He only thinks of the child.

"Eh, little Nell, little Nell!" he repeats, times without number. "Wake up, little Nell!"

Old Clo'es is so busy with the child in his arms that he does not hear a gentle tap at the door, nor see Lotty, who, surprised and alarmed, is bending over him now.

"Mester," she says, "that's never *your* little Nell, is it?"

Old Clo'es starts, and looks up at Lotty with a very troubled face.

"She's somebody's little un'," he says. "Somehow I took it as she was a little Nell; she looks like one! But maybe she's got another name. Lotty, I can't waken her, an' I'm afeard she's goin' to die!"

"*She'll* not die, mester," says Lotty wisely, as she peers into the little pale face of the child. "She's had somethin' to sleep her, very like. See, she's openin' her eyes now, mester. Eh, but she's a bonny little lass!"

And sure enough, as Old Clo'es looks down into the tiny face once more, a pair of large blue eyes meet his with a sleepy, wondering gaze. Then the tiny hands are poked into her eyes, and a shrill, bird-like voice calls out, "Mammie! mammie!"

"All right, little lovey, little Nell!" says Old Clo'es soothingly. "You've got Dad instead for a while. And you shall tell him all about mammie by-and-bye. Mammie's gone for a bit, little Nell. Never you mind!"

At first the child seems inclined to cry for her mother, but before she can pucker up her mouth for a good scream, she catches sight of the tea-things on the table, and instead of crying, she holds out her hands towards them, saying eagerly:

"Werry hung'y! so hung'y!"

"Eh, then!" says Old Clo'es, delighted, as he shuffles into the arm-chair by the table with his burden. "So little Nell wants her tea? an' little Nell shall have it!"

Fingers and teeth are soon hard at work, and Old Clo'es looks on, with his face all twinkling over with smiles, holding his great mug every now and then to her lips for a sip of tea.

"How ever did she come here, mester?" asks Lotty, who is also looking on with great interest.

"Well," says Old Clo'es solemnly, "she come without *her* knowin' it, an' without *me* knowin' it, an' that's just all I can tell you, Lotty! You see, she were done up in a bundle o' clo'es as a woman sell't me, an' I never knew nought about it until I unwrapped the bundle, an' there she were sleepin' like dead."

"I guess her mother wanted to get shut on her, mester," says Lotty, shaking her head safely. "There's a many like that in London. What ever'll you do with her, mester! You'll hev' to let the p'leece know!"

"I haven't much faith in they p'leece,"

answers Old Clo'es, doubtfully, drawing the child closer to him as he speaks; "I don't think I sall say aught to 'em about her."

"Then you'll a'vertise for her, I s'pose?" says Lotty.

"I couldn't make up my mind to comin' afore the public i' that a' way, Lotty. I've always been respec'able an' private. I shouldn't like my name to be spelled out i' the papers!"

"Then you'll hev' to get her into the House," says Lotty again.

"The House is a werry bad place for little lasses to grow up in, they say, Lotty. No, I couldn't send her there. I sall keep her while her mother comes for her, Lotty; an' she'll be my little lass—my little Nell come back!"

"Maybe her name's summut else, mester," suggests Lotty.

"She'll never mind me callin' her that," says Old Clo'es. "I couldn't bring my tongue to call her aught else."

## CHAPTER III.

#### THE ACCIDENT.

Days pass by, then weeks and months, but no one comes to claim "Little Nell," as Old Clo'es always calls her.

It seems as if Lotty was right when she said her mother must have "made off," after leaving her child in what she thought safe hands.

When Old Clo'es goes his rounds through the streets now, when it is bright and fine, he always leads little Nell by one hand, and her merry chatter cheers his dull way.

Little Nell is not a bit shy now; she never asks for her mother, and has already a warm place in her heart for "Dad," as he delights to have her call him. She shrinks from speaking of her own hard, wild, half-starved life in the streets. It is all past and gone now, and she is happy.

Little Nell's rags have been laid away in a box "against mother's return," Old Clo'es says; and the happy child is decked out in a red petticoat and plaid jacket, manufactured out of Old Clo'es' stores by Lotty's clever fingers. Lotty takes a lively interest in "the mester's little lass."

As for Old Clo'es himself, little Nell has wound herself so closely round his heart, that he cannot bear to think of the wrench it will be to part with her when mother comes. He even hopes at times that she never will come, and that hope grows stronger as days go by.

"You never fear *her*, mester!" says Lotty, decidedly. "*She'll* not come. Do you think she'd ever ha' parted wi' little Nell if she'd wanted her? An' it's a rare good thing for the child!"

"I don't like the thought o' my little Nell's mother bein' bad!" says Old Clo'es. "Maybe she hadn't no *real* mother after all."

"I'll tell you what, mester—it looks as if she come of gipsies, or some o' them magicdealin' folk. There's ever such a great mark on one shoulder as some one's made there."

"Waxinasin'?" suggests Old Clo'es.

"Nay, it ain't that," says Lotty decidedly. "It's a letter o' some sort, clear enough. Folks doesn't waxinate wi' letters, mester. An' little Nell says she minds how her mammie cut her shoulder a piece one day, and put stuff in it to make the place show. Her mammie cried about it, too, she said."

"It don't look like as if she was unkind, when she cried about it—do it, Lotty?" says Old Clo'es gently.

"Folks *can* cry," says Lotty, very meaningly. "I shouldn't 'spect she treated the child kind."

"Maybe not—maybe not," says Old Clo'es sadly. "Lotty, I don't well see how I could bring myself to part wi' my little Nell if her mother come an' wanted her. I reckon it 'ud go nigh to break my heart!"

"Never you fear, mester; *she'll* not trouble herself!" answers Lotty.

And Lotty's words seem likely to come

true. But one day in early spring, when the withered primroses have just begun to go about London in baskets, the old man had an alarm about little Nell.

He is buying a halfpenny bunch of primroses for her of a child in the street, when little Nell suddenly clings close to him, and gives a frightened cry.

Old Clo'es pays for the bunch, and then takes his little lass into a quiet corner.

"What is it, lovey? What ails my little Nell?" he asks softly.

Little Nell looks round her fearfully before she answers:

"Dad, it were *mother!* I see'd her ever so plain just round the corner. Oh, Dad, please don't let mother go for to take me back to the streets with her!"

"Never thee fear, little Nell!" whispers the old man soothingly. "Maybe it wasn't mother after all; and anyway she won't come for my little lass—I couldn't bear it!"

But little Nell can't put her fears away. All that day she clings close to Old Clo'es' side, and will not leave him even for a moment.

The old man makes up his mind that now he will never trust her out of his sight for long, lest she should be run away with, or at least frightened by seeing her mother again.

He will do his best to prevent the woman from finding out where her child lives, and so he takes care to go on his rounds, as far as possible, by a different road every day. He begs Lotty not to gossip with any of the neighbours about his little charge.

Lotty, too, fancies that she has seen a woman with a look of little Nell in her face loitering about Scrub's Alley, and seeming to be looking for some one or something. She warns little Nell not to play near the attic window, and never to sing when it is open, "fear mother 'ud hear, and come for her."

And little Nell readily obeys, for it is her greatest terror that mother may come and take her away from her happy life with the old man.

"Dad," says little Nell one day, as they are

out on their rounds together, "does everybody have a birthday—big folks an' all?"

"Well, yes, I s'pose so," answers Old Clo'es thoughtfully. "They all had a day to be born on, I s'pose. But there's a many doesn't reckon anythink of their birthdays, little Nell."

"But I'll reckon a lot on yours, Dad," says little Nell warmly. "When was you born, Dad?"

"Oh, a many years ago," answers Old Clo'es. "My mother used to mind the day for me once, and then my little Nell as was; but I've quite forgot, 'cept that there was wi'lets in the country hedges then."

"Then I'll *give* you a birthday, Dad," says little Nell; "an' it'll be in primrose-time. I think it sall be to-morrow. What's to-morrow, Dad?"

"To-morrow's Sunday, little Nell."

"Then the shops 'll be all shut. You must have somethin' nice for your birthday, Dad! Will you give me two halfpennies, an' let me go au' buy somethin' now?"

"What ever 'll you buy, little Nell? I've

got you, an' that's every bit all I want!" says the old man fondly. "I couldn't let thee go alone, little lovey, fear harm 'ud take thee."

"Just once, Dad—on'y once, 'cos it's goin' to be your birthday?" coaxes the child.

Old Clo'es stands still in the street, fumbles in his pocket, and brings out the old leather purse.

"There's three halfpennies for ye, little Nell. Well, you *are* a rich woman now, ain't you? Go an' buy summut very p'tickler good, an' Dad *will* be pleased! Take care of yerself, little lovey!"

The child trots off down the street, and Old Clo'es hobbles along after her. He can't trust himself to let his little lass quite out of his sight.

Little Nell is full of delight at her errand.

"Dear old Dad," she says to herself, "I will reckon on his birthday. He shall have ever such a nice one. I'll hide all them old bags, an' sit on 'em, an' Dad 'll have a real good holiday. Well, an' what 'll I buy for him? I think I'll have to go into all them fine shops, an' see what they've got fust. Dad'll be a rich man to-morrow. Eh, and just fancy Dad sayin' he liked me better than nothin' else! Well, I s'pose that's about the way I likes Dad!"

So she goes on, chattering to herself, as fast as her feet can go, down the street and across it.

Poor little Nell! As ill luck will have it, she catches her foot against a stone. Down she goes, and the halfpence fly far and wide. Nell scrambles after them, forgetting quite that she is in the middle of the street.

There is the noise of wheels, and a carriage is driving past full speed. There is no time for the coachman to pull up, and little Nell, picking up her precious coins, is just in its way. Old Clo'es is too far off to help her, or even to see the danger his darling is in.

Another second, and it will be too late.

Then a woman dashes up to little Nell, seizes her by the frock, and flings her roughly aside. The child is safe, but the wheels pass over the body of the poor woman who so bravely risked her life to save little Nell.

Little Nell picks herself up, crying and bruised, and makes the best of her way to "Dad."

A crowd soon gathers round the poor creature who lies still and bleeding on the ground. Two or three men are trying to lift her on to the unhinged frame of a door.

Lotty is just on her way to Scrub's Alley with the week's marketing in a basket on her arm. By dint of elbows and sharp basket-corners, she manages to edge her way into the very middle of the crowd to make out for herself what has happened.

"What is it?" asks Lotty of a girl standing near her.

"A accident," answers the girl. "There was a little lass as she throwed out o' the way o' the horse's feet, an' the conwayance went clean over *her*. They're for taking her to the hospital."

"Is she bad?" asks Lotty.

"Werry bad, I'd say. She'll never come round, if she ain't dead a'ready. See, they've got her up now! That's a Sister—that there one in grey. She's showin' 'em what to do."

"A Sister! What ever's that?" says Lotty. "Ain't she dressed queer!"

"Eh, there's a many of 'em all alike; Sisters o' Charity they call 'em. She's Sister Raphael. I knows her 'cos she nussed my aunt as was!"

The crowd begins to move on, and for one moment Lotty gets a sight of the bruised and bleeding face of the unhappy creature on the door-frame.

Though it is but for a moment, and the face is so bruised and cut, Lotty feels sure that it is no other than the woman who has so long been skulking about Scrub's Alley—little Nell's mother.

Then she stays no longer, but carries home the news almost joyfully to Old Clo'es and the child.

"Little Nell, thou need'st not be afraid, never no more, now!" she says, taking the child on her knee, and pressing it warmly to her heart. "Thou'lt never be forced to leave thy Dad an' Lotty as loves thee so!"

"Eh, but it's a fearsome thing, Lotty," says the old man sadly; "to think o' her bein' took so sudden like! It seems to come sort o' *near*, her dyin'—bein', as she was, my little Nell's mother."

"Little Nell!" cries Lotty, in sudden alarm; "what's thee done to thy nose? It's all cut ever so!"

"There was a woman as throwed her down i' the street, somehow, but I couldn't rightly make it out," says Old Clo'es.

"It was my birthday pennies, Dad. I was pickin' em up, an' a great woman took an' throwed me down on the stones," says little Nell.

"It was your mother, little Nell, I'll be bound!" cries Lotty. "Then that was what they was talking about—an' it was our little Nell! Mester, there must ha' been good in her, arter all, to try and save little Nell. I wonder if she knowed as it were little Nell."

"Eh, there's good in everybody somewheres, I reckon," says Old Clo'es.

"I wonder which o' them two places she's gone to, mester?"

"I dun'no," says Old Clo'es, shaking his head. "I can't rightly tell how they settles folk there. I've two books as tells summut about it, Lotty. I've had 'em give me ever sin' I was a little lad. There's my chrissen' name in't i' the fust pages, but I could no more read 'em, than I could fly! Maybe you'll larn to read some day, Lotty, an' then you shall let us hear summut out o' my book—my little lass an' me!"

"Mester," says Lotty, "as I was passin' by one o' them church places t'other day, I see'd a board stuck up wi' writin' on it. There was a many young lasses lookin' at it werry p'tickler; so says I, 'What be them words about?' 'Sure, an' it's the good Sisters,' says one. 'There's goin' to be a night-school started, joined to St. Mary's Church, an' everyone as likes may go for larnin'.' 'What Sisters is it?' says I; 'be they yourn?' 'Nay,' she says; 'they be the Sisters of Charity, wot nusses in the hospital, and teaches.' 'An' where be the larnin' place?' says I. 'Just agen the church—yon red buildin',' says the girl. And thinks I, 'Eh, I *should* love to go!' But then mother wouldn't never go for to pay money just for me to get a bit o' schoolin'."

"Well, Lotty," says Old Clo'es, after a moment's thought, "I've bin a-kinsiderin' o' late how I'm to get my little lass a bit o' larnin'. I shouldn't like to see her grow up iggerant like her old Dad. So, if you like, Lotty, an' your mother don't see no harm, I'll pay your goin' to school reg'lar, perwided you'll larn my little Nell all they've teached you yonder. Are ye willin', Lotty?"

Poor Lotty's eyes are fairly brimming over with happy tears, and she answers with a very choking voice :

"Oh, mester! I couldn't never thank ye enough if I was to begin now an' go on till I died!"

"There isn't no need to do it, neither!" Old Clo'es replies. "It's just a matter to settle betwixt you an' your mother."

And Lotty goes downstairs to settle it.

## CHAPTER IV.

### LOTTY'S LARNIN'.

"You an' the mester's made up your minds, an' wants me to set my seal to it; that's it, is it?" grumbles Mrs. Walker, when Lotty, with a face beaming all over with delight, has asked her leave to go to school. "You'll leave *me* to do all your work, while you're gadding about, stuffin' your head with all manner of nonsense, I suppose?"

Lotty's bright face is clouding over, and she twists her apron nervously in her fingers as she says:

"Oh, *please*, mother, *don't* say 'No.' I do want to go an' learn bad, an' it does seem such a fine chance, as the mester has promised to pay. We didn't settle it atwixt us without you, mother. He said as it was for you an' me to settle. And, indeed, mother, I'll get up long afore it's light an' do the work if you'll only let me go—indeed I will!"

"And waste no end o' candle light, I'll be bound!" grumbles her mother. "Say no more about it, child; and I'll see what yer father says when he comes in."

Lotty brightens again at her mother's last words. Her father is a good-tempered, rosy-cheeked little costermonger, and if he has had a good day with the barrow, and brought home money in his pocket, he is pretty sure to give her leave to go to school.

So it turns out.

Jonathan Walker hears what his wife has to say about Lotty, and replies that "he thinks it 'ud be a nice bit o' change for the girl." So Mrs. Walker gives in, and Lotty is to go.

And what preparations Lotty makes, to be sure! Her face is scrubbed to such a degree that it has become a dangerous rival to the one pewter mug on the parlour chimney-piece. Her limp hair is plastered smoothly down round her long, thin face. Her frock is patched, darned, and improved to the highest possible pitch of improvement, considering that it came, to begin with, from one of Old

Clo'es' bundles. Thus dressed and got up, Lotty starts to get her first "bit o' larnin'."

It is almost dark, for Scrub's Alley boasts not a lamp. Only the tallow candles in the windows cast a flickering light on to the pavement. Neither moon nor stars are up.

The streets beyond the alley are better off for light, and Lotty soon finds her way to the red building where the night-school is to be held.

A pleasant-looking girl opens the door for poor, shy Lotty, who goes into a well-lighted room with an uncomfortable feeling of being at once too big and too small.

There are a great many people in the room, of all ages and sizes, sitting on benches before long tables, all so busy with book and slate that they do not even see Lotty come in. Lotty takes courage, and ventures further in.

The very same Sister, whom Lotty saw on the day of the accident, comes to meet her.

Lotty curtsies very low, and looks very much frightened.

"Tell me your name, dear, and don't be

frightened," the Sister says, in such a kind voice that Lotty feels much less afraid.

"Lotty, please, Sister,—Lotty Walker."

Then Lotty looks on with great interest while Sister Raphael writes her name in a book.

"And have you ever been to school before?" she asks next.

"No, Sister, and I don't know nothin', please," says Lotty humbly.

"Never mind, dear! You will soon if you take pains. Come and sit at this table, and begin at once."

It is not Sister Raphael, but another Sister whose name she does not know, to whose care Lotty is given. At first she is too much taken up with looking round the room, at the pictures on the wall, the other scholars, and the nuns with their strange grey dresses and good, kind faces, that the lesson does not get on very fast.

Then Lotty thinks of Old Clo'es and little Nell. She ought to know such a lot before she goes home to-night. Lotty pulls herself together, and works away at those queer-looking letters with right good will.

By the time the lesson is over Lotty has most of the alphabet by heart, and the nun gives her a small book to take home with her, so that she may know them all by next time.

There is just a short prayer and a hymn before school closes. Lotty kneels and stands as she sees the rest do, but the words of the "Hail Mary" have no meaning to her, poor child!

When Lotty gets home, she finds Old Clo'es waiting for her with his little Nell on his knee, and the candle lighted on the table.

"Thou'st been a long time, Lotty," he says. "Did thee get on well? an' was the folks good to thee? Me an' my little Nell's been expectin' you of a great while; she's gettin' werry sleepy! Give her her lessin, an' we'll put her in her bed."

Lotty brings out the precious book she has been given, and little Nell's voice and finger follow Lotty's down the alphabet. The old man's eyes twinkle and glisten with delight and pride at his darling's performance.

"A sugar-stick fro' the shop if she's a good little lass," he coaxes between smiles, as little Nell's attention begins to flag, and the golden head nods drowsily over the book.

And little Nell does her best, much to Lotty's satisfaction and her own.

"She shall have her sugar-stick to-morrow, she shall," says Old Clo'es, as they put the tired child to bed.

"Well, Lotty!" says Old Clo'es, when the little one is already fast asleep on her pillow; "how's it all gone on?"

"Oh, very well indeed, mester," says Lotty cheerily. "There wasn't nothink to be afeard on, though them Sisters does look queer-dressed—like a lot o' grey mice."

"Well," says Old Clo'es, "I make no doubt they was all right enough. You wimmin-folk always *does* seem to me queer-dressed, whatever you has on; an' I s'pose *I* ought to know if anybody does! You an' me's quite set 'fashion i' Scrub's Alley and Battle's Court, Lotty!"

"Ay," says Lotty, nodding her head proudly. "Well, mester, an' then I went on larnin' ever so hard wi' a Sister, till it was time for to shut up; an' then—well, they all set to doin' the funniest thing as ever I see'd! They threw their arms about a bit, an' then they all knelt down on the floor—an' Sister Raphael at the top o' the room began somethin' about 'Maries' an' all the rest took it up an' finished it. Then they singed a hymn ever so pretty—an' that was all about 'Mary' too."

"Maybe she's some grand lady as set the school goin'," suggested Old Clo'es.

"It seems to me she have summut to do wi' all on 'un, by how hearty-like they sang, and said them words arter Sister Raphael," says Lotty. "I wonder if it's her who's St. Mary at the church?"

"I shouldn't be s'prised if she was," says Old Clo'es. "Lotty, you remembers them books I telled ye I had giv' me when I was a little lad? I've dusted 'em, an' laid 'em out on the table. As soon as you can spell out a page, we'll have 'em—my little Nell an' me. You see I'm gettin' a werry old man, Lotty. I'm not p'tickler to a year or so, but I can't be far off eighty; an' little Nell's mother bein' took, as I s'pose, so sudden, makes a man think. I don't know what there is in them books, but anyway there's somethink as helped my poor mother to die comfor'ble. An' I'd like to know what it is, Lotty."

"Sister—her as they call Sister Raphael—says I shall learn quick, mester," says Lotty. "An' I'll say the same o' little Nell. She got them letters werry well, did little Nell!"

"An' she'll get the sugar-stick to-morrow, she will!" says Old Clo'es, with a loving look at the golden curls resting on the pillow.

## CHAPTER V.

### ST. MARY'S CATECHISM CLASS.

"It's all *Saint Mary*. I'd like to know who she is, ever so!" says Lotty; "only I haven't the face to ask."

"What is it now, Lotty?" asks Old Clo'es.

"Well, it's a werry nice thing," says Lotty, eagerly. "There's goin' to be a Sunday afternoon catechissen class, as well as night-school, for all as cares to go athout payin'. I don't rightly know what it is, but it's summut good. Mester, will thee an' little Nell go along wi' me?"

"Would they let me an' my little lovey in?" asks Old Clo'es, eagerly; "ain't us two too old an' too young?"

"I've axed—I've axed Sister Raphael," says Lotty; "an' says she, 'We'll be werry glad to see 'em, Lotty,' quite hearty!"

"To be sure, it's werry considerin' like of the Sisters," says Old Clo'es. "What 'll you say, little Nell?"

"We'll go with Lotty, please, Dad; it'll be fine!" says little Nell, joyfully.

"Then of course we will!" says Old Clo'es; "you may reckon on us, Lotty!"

Lotty's reading lessons have got on apace. She almost feels her store of learning too great a burden at times. Little Nell, too, knows her letters, and can even spell little words with a fair amount of prompting. Old Clo'es has laid in a bountiful store of sugar-sticks for his little lovey's daily lesson.

Lotty has even begun to spell out the precious books. One turns out to be a "Garden of the Soul."

"We haven't not come to no flowers yet," says Lotty; "but maybe they're to come furder on. There's Mary again, mester—sort o' speaking to her. I wonder what it all means!"

The other book is an old Douay Bible. Lotty spells it out chapter after chapter, most untiringly, even to the long genealogies, through which she flounders bravely.

"I'm not much wiser for it, mester, be you?" she says at last. They have reached the Apocalypse. "An' it's all strange creatures now, and things as people don't never see. What do it all mean?"

"There's good in them books *somewheres*," says Old Clo'es, confidently; "an' we'll go back'ards an' forrards till we come to it. To my thinkin' even them namey parts beats the newspapers as the old fellow in the public reads out of an evening. There's somethin' oncommon about it; an' it'll sound grand, I make no doubt, Lotty, when you haven't to stop so long at them big words. Let's take the 'Garding' for a piece, Lotty; it's better to make out nor the other."

Another time little Nell asks again for the wonderful story of the Birth at Bethlehem. They can all understand a little of that. The little child creeps softly round to Dad's side, and listens with blue eyes full of wonder and delight as Lotty follows the verses with her thumb.

"Do you hear, Dad? It was born in a stable, with the cows and the horses! Eh, what a birthday to have! An' it didn't have a bed nor nothin'. It hadn't even rags, an' its mother laid it in the manger. I'd like to ha' seen that little baby, Dad!"

"I wonder when that there happened?" says Old Clo'es, nodding towards the book which lies open on Lotty's knee. "I s'pose they know, but it must ha' bin a good while ago, for that book was my mother's afore it were mine. I reckon the child 'll be a werry old man by now if He's still alive even, Lotty!"

"He goes on to the end of the book, and out of it," says Lotty; "for I've looked. It finished up wi' somethin' about His comin' to see folks, an' everybody seein' Him; an' it doesn't speak as if He'd come yet."

"It was a werry poor place for Him to be in, was that stable," comments Old Clo'es, "all the while when He was a great king, as I s'pose. I wonder they couldn't find Him better lodgings! He'll most like' be wearin' the gold crown as was His by rights now, Lotty!"

"Ay," answers Lotty. "Mester, that was *Mary* again as was *His* mother. Is it *our* St. Mary, I wonder?"

"It may be, Lotty; it may be!" says Old Clo'es, thoughtfully.

Sunday comes at last, and proud Lotty leads the old man with little Nell between them into the school-room.

"It be a very beautiful place, for sure!" whispers Old Clo'es, as he takes his seat beside Lotty. "I don't s'pose little Nell's ever seen such a beautiful place afore, Lotty—picters an' all!"

I am not going to take you to the Catechism-class. You know what it is like, for you have been to many in your lives, and I hope will go to many more. Our lives must wind round and round our Catechism if we want them to be all they ought.

That night Lotty slips away to Old Clo'es' attic as early as she can, for a talk over the wonderful event of the day.

She finds him sitting by the bedside of "his little lass," as he calls her, watching her peaceful sleep with a beautifully soft, tender look on his face. He seems to have been crying a very little, too, for there are wet places here and there on little Nell's pillow.

He looks up when Lotty comes in, and says gently:

"Little Nell was too tired to sit up for thee, Lotty. I had to put her in her bed at last, for she a'most went asleep in my arms. Eh, Lotty, lass! thy face is as bright as summer sunshine. What's come t' 'ee?"

"I've need look glad, mester!" cries Lotty. "I've never been so happy in all my life as I am to-night—never nothin' nowhere near it."

"It's what the good Sister tell't us to-day, I s'pose?" says Old Clo'es. "Is you goin' to do as she says, Lotty?"

"In course I be," rejoins Lotty. "I've let father and mother know, too; an' they're set a-thinkin'. I'ze goin' to stay to-morrow night for 'structions, an' then I'ze goin' to kinfesshin."

"It's werry hard thing to do, is that, Lotty, seems to me," says Old Clo'es, "more in 'spec'ller when you've got a weight o' years behind your back, an' a deal in 'em as ain't over an' above right."

"But it'll have to be *some time*, she says, mester," says Lotty: "t' judgmen', you know! An' it's better back'ard nor forrard. I don't like bad things to look to."

"Well, you'll try it fust off, Lotty," says Old Clo'es, " an' then me an' my little Nell 'll follow arter. *She'll* not have the 'ard part of it, poor little lamb."

"I'd reckon on it's makin' a body feel lighter an' comfor'bler arterwards," says Lotty.

"Lotty, shall we have a bit o' the ' Garding' to-night ?" says Old Clo'es, "just to go to bed on? Seems to me it'll be more understandabler than it was now."

"Ay, mester," says Lotty gladly. "An' I'm main pleased to know a bit about her as they call Mary. It's the same as is everywhere. And she's *His* mother as was born in the stable. An' He's God, an' He loves us, an' takes care on us—you an' me, an' little Nell, an' all on us! An' we've got to tell Him everythin', an' to ask Him for just what we want. An' He's everywhere, but we can't see Him; an' there's nothin' He can't do. My! ain't He awfu' grand, mester?"

"Ay;" answers Old Clo'es, "but seems to me there's not so much to be done fearin' as lovin' Him. He ain't one o' them grand folks as has carriages, an' won't look on you, case you 'ain't werry good cov'rin', nor manners neither, for the matter o' that. Leastways, it don't appear so."

"What 'll we have out o' the 'Garding,' mester?" asks Lotty.

"That 'ere little piece as we had to-day, Lotty," says Old Clo'es; "I've took a strange fancy to that. It's not long, but there's a deal in it. An' it's about '*Our death*,' Lotty," Old Clo'es adds in a lower voice. "I must begin to be thinkin' about that."

So the old man and Lotty kneel by the little one's bedside, and say together their first prayer—the Hail Mary.

## CHAPTER VI.

#### LITTLE NELL'S BIRTHDAY.

It is a bright sunshiny May morning. People feel it even in the dreary courts, lanes, and alleys of the city.

In the grand streets and squares gaily dressed folk are airing themselves, and in the parks bands of happy children play and rejoice in the warmth and brightness of the day.

Dim, dark, and dirty as Scrub's Alley is, for two at least who live in it, to-day is a feast-day, marked out in red letters from all the rest of the year.

It is little Nell's birthday. Not knowing his little lassie's real birthday, Old Clo'es has made over to her the birthday of his first little Nell, kept with so much rejoicing fifty years ago. It shall be just the same for his little lovey's birthday now, Old Clo'es makes

## Little Nell's Birthday.

up his mind, not a bit less of a red-letter day. He set his wits to work, planning what shall be done to celebrate it, quite a week beforehand.

As good luck will have it, that important matter is settled for the old man, partly by chance, partly by little Nell herself.

Three days before her birthday the old man, with his little lass's hand in his, is going his usual round. His customers are mostly in the very poor parts of the city, but to-day little Nell begs so hard that dad will take her into the big, grand streets where she can see the gaily decked-out shops, the horses and carriages, and all the busy sights and sounds that the old man can't find it in his heart to say no. They wander down a long, straight street, and Old Clo'es listens with delight to the little child's chatter about all she sees.

"What's that beautiful place, with gold letters an' glass doors, dad?" asks little Nell, stopping before a gin-palace.

"It's a werry bad place, little Nell," says Old Clo'es. "Never you mind it. It's like a cobweb to catch silly flies in."

"There, Dad! see that beautiful carriage, an' the horses with bells ringin'! Oh, Dad, wouldn't you like to ride so? An' there's a little girl in the carriage no bigger than me, an' dressed ever so grand!"

"I like you best in your old clothes, little Nell," says the old man, sighing. "Don't you get wishing for what you can't have. That's werry bad!"

"Eh, but I should love a new frock, ever so, Dad!" says little Nell; "a nice un wi' buttings i' the front, an' a real pocket, Dad!"

"Eh, would ye then, little Nell!" says Old Clo'es, with a twinkle in his eyes.

"Dad, Dad!" cries little Nell, in great excitement. "See, there's a woman callin' yer! She stands i' that doorway up the steps. What ever can she be wantin'? Who is it, Dad?"

"Not any werry persinal acquaintince, little Nell," says Old Clo'es. "Maybe it's a new custimer."

And Clo'es, leading his little lass by the hand, goes to see.

He is right. The woman has a large bundle of children's clothing to sell. Old Clo'es makes a very good bargain with her for them.

"Who'd ever ha' thought o' comin' this a way for a custimer, little Nell?" the old man says, in a tone of great glee, as they go on their way. "Thee's summut of a wise woman, I reckon, little lovey!"

"See, Dad!" cries little Nell; "why is them window-shutters all closed where yon woman lives? Is it to keep out the sunshine, Dad?"

But for once in his life Old Clo'es neither hears nor answers his little lass. He is busy reckoning up in his own mind what these clothes will sell for. He has got them very cheap, and yet some of them are almost new. One little frock—a bright blue print, daintily trimmed with frills and braid—Old Clo'es has already singled out from the rest. It will just fit his little Nell, and shall be her birthday present!

When the grand day comes round, Old Clo'es, with a height of solemnity befitting the occasion, presents his little lass with the pretty blue dress.

"Eh, Dad," says little Nell, when she has half smothered the old man with kisses and thanks, "if I'm a wise woman, you's certinly a wise man. It's just the veriest nicest frock as could ever ha' been. Fancy you gettin' it for me! Dress me up, so as Lotty 'll see me grand, please, Dad!"

Old Clo'es' fingers tremble with joy as he fastens the many hooks that secure his darling's new garment. His eyes fairly brim over with pride and admiration when he sets her on the table to be looked at with her toilet complete.

And surely never was there a prettier picture! Little Nell's golden hair falls in thick waves over her shoulders; the deep, full blue of her eyes is almost a match for the frock she wears; and the soft pink colour that shyness and pleasure have brought to her pale cheeks adds to the beauty of the child.

Of course Lotty must be brought in to see her. And in slips lean, awkward Lotty, with a great many birthday wishes and kisses, and a wonderful parcel, bound round many times with scarlet worsted, which she pokes into the hands of the queen of the day.

"Open it, little Nell—it's from Lotty!" cries the delighted girl. And when the tiny fingers, with Lotty's eager help, have untied the many knots that secure it, out comes a small paper-covered book, gloriously sprinkled with pictures of unearthly cats, with large-type tales of cat-life underneath them.

"*Well* now," says Lotty, "*isn't* that beautiful, little Nell? I bought it at the shop, yesterday afternoon. It was 'ard not to show it to ye there an' then! Isn't them pusses live-like?"

For all answer little Nell throws her arms round Lotty's neck, and kisses her half a hundred times. Lotty receives each kiss as if it were a queenly gift.

"We'll reckon on Lotty's birthday, won't we, dad?" says little Nell.

"Ay, *that* we will, little lovey," says Old Clo'es heartily.

"Now, what are you goin' to do for her to-day, mester?" inquires Lotty, when the child has gone back to her cats. "You're never goin' your rounds on her birthday, are yer, mester?"

"I'm going to do just what little Nell likes," answers Old Clo'es, rubbing his hands with delight. "I'm goin' to give myself a whole holiday to-day—an' what'll little Nell like to do?"

"Please, Dad, take me into the big streets again in my new frock," begs little Nell, coming up to the old man's side, and laying her golden head on his knee, in a coaxing way she has.

"You want to show your frock to all the grand folks," says Old Clo'es, with just a trifle of sadness in his tone; "but, don't you know, they'll never look or care what a poor little girl like you's got on."

However, little Nell is bent upon going, so Old Clo'es takes her. She is very soon disappointed, as the old man knew she would be. Nobody seems to notice her or her blue frock, any more than if she had only her old clothes on. Then Old Clo'es takes her into a cook shop, and buys her a bun.

Somehow little Nell is soon tired to-day, and when they leave the shop to go home she asks pitifully—"Please, Dad, carry me a while!"

"Thee's werry tired, little Nell!" says Old Clo'es, as he takes her in his arms. "It's been a werry excitin' mornin' for my little lass. I reckon you've never had another such day, little Nell—what wi' the bun, an' the new frock, an' the cats in the book—have you?"

"Never, Dad!" says little Nell, contentedly shutting her eyes as he carries her home. "I reckon heaven 'll be summut like to-day—birthdays always goin' on. White robes and crowns there'll be there; won't there, Dad? But we couldn't wear them in Scrub's Alley, 'cos they'd soon be black; wouldn't they, Dad? Will the grand folks care in heaven, Dad?"

"I reckon they'll care a deal more for the likes of us than they do here," answers Old Clo'es. "Our Lord 'll be there, little Nell; an' He wasn't very far different from you an' me once. He'll show 'em as they ought to care."

"I should like to go to heaven, Dad!" says little Nell.

"Not yet a while, little Nell. I 'spect you'll

go straight there when you does go; but I'll be going first, so as things 'll be comfor'ble afore you come."

"We'll all go together, dad, you an' me, an' Lotty, an' p'r'aps Mr. Walker. I axed himself yesterday if he wouldn't see the priest, and get made a good man, an' go to Mass along of us o' Sundays; an' I axed him if he didn't want to go to heaven? He looked quite funny, dad, an' sort o' cried, and said he'd see about it; he never had before."

"Do they have birthdays in heaven, Dad?" asks little Nell presently.

"I've never heard so," answers Old Clo'es thoughtfully.

"Maybe they've birthdays all the year round!" suggests little Nell.

The old man is getting very weary with his heavy burden, but the little tired child in his arms does not offer to walk, so he carries her until they enter the dismal alley once more.

Even then she pleads wearily—

"Carry me up them long stairs, please, Dad."

And Old Clo'es obeys her. Once in their

attic, he lays her on the bed—just as she is, in her precious blue frock, and in her hood. Even there she never opens her eyes—little, tired, sleepy eyes!—and before the old man has left her side, she is fast asleep, with a dark patch of red in each cheek, and everywhere else quite pale and white—even to her lips.

All through her birthday little Nell sleeps—on, on—as if she never would wake again.

Night comes, and she never opens her eyes.

Old Clo'es begins to grow very anxious about his little lass, and very heavy at the heart, until, kneeling before the plain black crucifix hanging now on the naked wall, he takes all the load of his troubles and fears to that loving Heart which is ever ready to listen to us.

Then he goes to rest peacefully beside little Nell, feeling sure that he and his little lass are in very safe keeping.

## CHAPTER VII.

### VERY ILL.

When Old Clo'es awakes next morning, he sees little Nell sitting upright in bed, talking very wildly and fast of the birthday joys of yesterday. Her face is flushed purple, and there is a strange, dull look in the blue eyes that stare so vacantly at the old man, while she chatters away, not knowing what she is saying.

Old Clo'es speaks to her again and again, but little Nell pays no heed. She doesn't seem even to know he is there, though she never takes her eyes off him.

"Little Nell, my little Nell! You're never goin' to be ill?" wails Old Clo'es piteously. "God 'll surely never let my little lass get ill, an' be took away from me! She's all I have on this earth."

His next thought is to call Lotty to his help. He lays his little lass gently down on the pillow, and calls her through the flooring.

Lotty looks at little Nell and then at Old Clo'es with a very sorrowful face.

"She's goin' to be werry ill, mester," she says. "How ever 'll you be able to nuss her?"

"Almighty God knows all about it, an' He'll help me," falters Old Clo'es. "Lotty, do you think your mother 'ud come an' see what's right to be done for my little lass? I can do for her right enough, if I only know what."

"I'm sure mother 'll come!" says Lotty more brightly. "Mother's took ever such a likin' for little Nell, an' she'll know all about what to do."

Mrs. Walker only takes one look at the child's flushed face before she says that she has got scarlet fever.

"A nice thing to have in the house!" she grumbles, "an' no knowin' how long it'll be afore we get shut of it!"

But as she busies herself settling little Nell comfortably in bed, the woman's face and manner soften. Old Clo'es folds up the poor little garments with the gay birthday frock, and lays them away in a box until his little lass is well enough to wear them again. Then he waits to do what he can to help.

"I don't see that you're much good, mester," says Mrs. Walker, not unkindly. "You'd best go an' fetch a lemon or two from the shop, an' then Lotty shall make a cool drink. I'll see to the child while you're away; she's a'most parched wi' thirst!"

By the time Old Clo'es comes back from his errand, little Nell has fallen asleep. It is a heavy, restless sleep, in which she tosses to and fro wildly, so that the bed-clothes must be smoothed every now and then.

"I don't see much use in callin' in doctors, an' such-like," Lotty's mother says sharply before she goes. "They only help to pile up bills, an' when you've a body ill, you don't want nothin' extry i' that line. I happen to know pretty much all that ought be done in fever cases, an' if you don't, why, I s'pose you ain't too proud to learn, mester? I've took a fancy to that child somehow. She's a nice little thing, an' if you want anythin' doin' for her, I'll do it: remember that!"

Lotty's mother is one of those people who hide a very kind heart under a very rough, unpleasant manner. It always seems such a pity to me when that is the case, for hidden hearts are apt to freeze for want of use, whilst open ones grow warmer and larger every day!

Mrs. Walker nurses little Nell herself, giving Old Clo'es rest whenever she can. A few days later, when the fever is at the highest, and it needs strong hands to hold the feverish child in bed, the kind landlady never leaves her. And when the crisis is passed at last, and little Nell begins to mend slowly, even Old Clo'es' heart can hardly be more glad than that of Lotty's mother.

When no one is there to see her, the good woman sits by little Nell's bedside, cooling her hot hands and forehead, and speaking soft, tender words to soothe her, just as a gentle mother might. It is only when others are by that her heart goes down into its shell, and she puts on her old sharp manner once more.

"Mester," she says one day, "you bought that lot o' clo'es as little Nell's frock was in of a woman in a big house up steps in yon street off Battle's Court; didn't you, now?"

"Ay," answers Old Clo'es; "an' what o' that, missus?"

"Do you mind that the shutters was every one closed, an' the house a'most shut up, mester?" questions Mrs. Walker.

"Well, I can't be too sure," says Old Clo'es, thoughtfully; "I didn't give it much notice. A werry respec'able-lookin' woman-servant sell't me 'em."

"More's the pity as you don't look afore you leap!" says Lotty's mother, grimly; "you'd 'a' saved this precious child a deal if you'd looked *then!*"

"What d'ye mean, missus?" gasps forth Old Clo'es. The terrible truth is beginning to dawn upon him.

"There was *fever in them clo'es,* an' you brought it an' giv'd it yerself to your little lass," says Lotty's mother, sharply. "It were a fine birthday present, that were! That house was shut up, an' the family as lived there, some flitted an' some dead. There, there, mester! Don't go an' take on so! You've no more nerve than a cat. What's done can't be undone."

"If my little Nell had died, I should ha' killed her, then!" murmurs the old man, shuddering. "Thank God, she's comin' round! If she'd ha' died, an' I'd come to know that, it 'ud ha' killed me right away. Oh, my little Nell! my own little pretty lovey!"

"I never reckoned on you bein' so cut up, mester," says Lotty's mother more kindly; "if I had, I'd never ha' breathed a word to you. Little Nell's comin' round all right, mester; so you just cheer up!"

But somehow all that day Old Clo'es can't shake off the feeling that he has, without knowing it, been the cause of his little lass's illness. Besides this, he feels low and unwell in himself. A great drowsiness is stealing over him, and he owns to having a sort of longing to go to sleep for years, and be really rested.

He is pale and worn out, too. His cheeks are no longer like russet apples, and his step is very slow and tired.

Mrs. Walker thinks the watching and trouble have been too much for him, and she makes him lie down and try to sleep by little Nell's side. He looks a very old, old man as he lies there, sleeping heavily—older than she has seen him look before. But then these last days have been very hard for him.

Old Clo'es is something more than tired and worn out.

"Poor old man! He's got it, sure enough," Mrs. Walker says to Lotty next morning, after a night spent by little Nell's side. "He don't know nothin' wot's said to him, an' he burns wi' fever."

"What ever shall you do, mother?" asked Lotty.

"That I don't know," answers her mother sharply; "if I did, I should do it, an' say no more! He's an old man to nurse here alone, is Old Clo'es. If he don't come round, who's to say as I've dealt fair and true with him?"

"There's the hospital, mother," says Lotty. "Shall I see Sister Raphael? I know they'll take Old Clo'es in if they've room."

"Well, I do think it'll be as well for you to go there, an' axe to see one o' the Sisters, Lotty," says Mrs. Walker. "He'd be well looked to there, an' they does take in 'fectious cases, I b'lieve. Tell 'em about him—the fever, an' all that—and look sharp back, Lotty!"

So Old Clo'es goes to the hospital that very

day in a covered cart, wrapped closely in blankets.

Little Nell is brought in for a last kiss, before the cart rumbles away slowly over the uneven flags.

"Dad, Dad! Won't you speak?" pleads the poor child, bending over the old man, who does not seem to know her, and stroking him gently with her two hands. "You're never goin' to let 'em take you away wi'out sayin' 'Good-bye' to little Nell, are you, Dad?" she goes on piteously.

"Never you mind, little Nell!" coaxes Lotty; "he don't rightly understand. The good Sister 'll nurse him better, an' then you an' me'll go an' see him i' the hospital."

"Dad won't speak! Dad doesn't know little Nell!" wails the poor little girl. "It's little Nell, Dad. She's come to say 'Good-bye'!"

Lotty cannot bear to see the child's grief any longer. She carries her away, and tries her best to comfort her.

"Dad 'll come back soon quite better, an'

then they'll all be happy together again—little Nell 'ud see! Only they must say their prayers werry hard till he comes back."

Lotty goes to the hospital every day after this to ask how Old Clo'es is, but there is never any very good news to carry home to little Nell, who always sends a loving message that Dad cannot know or hear, for he is still unconscious.

Day after day Old Clo'es lies on his hospital bed, knowing no one, knowing nothing—not even that he is very, very ill.

And all those days the nurse who has care of him under the Sister scarcely leaves him. She watches over him as tenderly as a mother.

Sometimes when Old Clo'es speaks in his wanderings of "his little Nell; his little lass as is so werry ill; little Nell as God had give him when he lost his own little girl!" the nurse fairly breaks down, puts up her apron to her eyes, and sobs aloud.

At last, after a long, long sleep, Old Clo'es comes to himself once more—still very weak, very ill—but a little better for the time.

"My little Nell!" are his first words, spoken in a low whisper.

Nurse Mary brings her ear close down to his mouth.

"My little Nell!" Old Clo'es says again; "she'll be wantin' me ever so, will my little Nell! When 'll they let me go back to her?"

"Not just yet; you must be patient a little while," replies the nurse soothingly. "She'll be comin' to see you by-and-by. The porter told me there's a little girl comes every day to ask how you are."

"That 'll be Lotty," says Old Clo'es, half to himself. "She's a werry good girl, is Lotty. She'll be good to my little lass while I'm away."

Then he shuts his eyes and says no more for a while. He feels perfectly content and happy.

"Our dear Lord's been werry good to me," he is thinking. "He's werry mother-like wi' His children! This be a uncommon nice place to be ill in, wi' the beautiful picters, an' the soft bed, an' all you wants, an' a kind body to take care on yer! I'm right glad it was Our Lord's will, an' they brought me here.

P'r'aps Our Lady 'll be good enough to thank Him for me proper. I ain't much of a hand, more in 'spec'ller sin' I'm growed so weak."

Next day Old Clo'es is well enough to see Lotty with little Nell for a few minutes.

When Lotty carries the joyful news home, poor little Nell cries for very joy. Arrayed in her best frock to do him honour, and holding Lotty's hand, she trots to the hospital to see Dad again.

And there, in a little room by himself, lies Old Clo'es, just propped up a little by pillows —so worn, and pale, and ill; a very shadow of his old self—but looking, oh, so happy, to see his little Nell once more !

Lotty lifts up the little girl for a kiss, and she throws her arms fondly round the old man's neck.

"When's you comin' home, Dad ?" she asks eagerly. "Lotty an' me 'ud nuss you ever so! An' I've been wantin' you ever since you went away ! Dad, we *did* reckon on comin' to see you ! Now tell Dad, Lotty."

"Mester," says Lotty solemnly, "little

Nell's been just as good as she could be—you can't think how good she's been! She fretted a bit at first, but when I tell'd her Dad 'ud grieve if she cried, she didn't cry no more. An' she has been prayin' hard for Dad to get better, has little Nell!"

"She's Dad's good little lass, is little Nell!" whispers Old Clo'es, and little Nell's face crimsons like a bonny rosebud at his loving words.

"You'll tell your mother, Lotty," says Old Clo'es, "as she'll find what money I've got left in a bag in my cupboard. Little Nell knows where—she'll find it. Missus must take all for the little lass's keep an' care-takin'-of while I'm away. Tell her as I never can thank her enough for doing so kind by little Nell."

"You don't think nothin' about that, mester!" says Lotty earnestly. "Mother 'ud never touch a penny o' yourn for seein' to the little un. Why, she loves her like her own, she says!"

"Tell her I'll thank her for it when I can," says Old Clo'es, very gratefully; "I don't feel to be able to say much now. But she must take the money, Lotty. I couldn't bear to have my little Nell takin' from other folks wi'out payin' back, you see. The goodness and kindness nobody can ever pay!"

The time is up; Old Clo'es is tired; Lotty and little Nell must go.

"Bring her again to-morrow, Lotty," says the kind nurse. "Sister Julian has given leave."

"Why," cries Lotty, looking into the nurse's face, "you are Mary Baker, aren't you—as was at night-school along wi' me?"

"Yes," answers Nurse Mary, colouring a little. "How do you come to know my name?"

"Oh," says Lotty, "I know it well enough. You used to have such a terrible sad face, an' Sister Raphael asked us all to pray for you, 'cos you'd got a great trouble to bear. You'd lost somebody as you loved werry much. But you look a deal happier now. Is the trouble gone yet?"

"Not quite gone yet. Will you go on prayin' for me, Lotty?"

"Ay, *that* I will!" Lotty promises gladly;

"an' I have—a many times. I know it'll all come right at last!"

"An' little Nell 'll pray for you, too! Little Nell 'll say a 'Hail Mary,' for 'oo every day," says the child, stroking Nurse Mary's hand softly.

Mary Baker stoops down and kisses the little fair face, and cries softly for a moment; but you can see that they are not sad tears.

"Mind you come again to-morrow!" she says, as the two children leave the room.

## CHAPTER VIII.
### LITTLE NELL'S MOTHER.

AGAIN and again Lotty and little Nell come to see the old man in the hospital, and each time the child asks pleadingly:

"Dad, aren't you goin' to be better soon?"

"Patience, little Nell!" Old Clo'es always answers. "I'm gettin' on just every bit as fast as I can. We must wait our dear Lord's will, little lovey!"

But Old Clo'es doesn't get up his strength.

It even seems that he grows weaker day by day.

One morning Nurse Mary tells the children, very sadly, that they must not come again to see the old man for some days—he cannot bear the excitement.

Old Clo'es himself feels that he is growing weaker. Except for his little lass's sake, he does not mind; but he would like to live for little Nell, if it were God's will.

"She'd be werry lonesome if her dad was took," he says to himself. "The world's a werry cold, hard place for little lasses to grow up in alone. Dear Lord, Thou wouldst never let my little Nell be left alone—it 'ud break her heart!"

And a gentle voice seems to promise Old Clo'es that little Nell will not be left alone.

A day comes when Old Clo'es feels weaker and more ill than ever. His breath comes so hardly, and there is a strange swimming in his head.

Nurse Mary props him up gently with pillows. For a while that eases him, and he thanks her with his soft smile—sweeter and gentler now than ever.

"Nurse," he says faintly, "I don't think I'm long for this world now, am I?"

"I think you will not be here very long," Nurse Mary says. "They told me to tell you the truth. Are you afraid to die?"

"Not esac'ly afraid," says Old Clo'es. "Our Lord is werry good, an' I'm always prayin' to Him, an' asking His Blessed Mother to pray that He'll do just what He likes wi' me, an' make me glad to have it done. I don't 'spect I'll go Home straight. There'll be a waitin' time fust. I've a many things to set right, I know, atwixt the Lord and me, as I can't mind of now. But Lotty an' little Nell 'll not forget to pray for me. Afore I go I want to thank you for all your kindness, Nurse. You've been good to me, Nurse, werry good! an' Our Lord 'll be sure to reward you for it. I axe Him every day!"

"You must tell me if there's anything I can do for you," says Nurse Mary kindly. "Tell me anythin' you wish."

"You are werry good!" whispers Old Clo'es gratefully. "There is just somethin' as I wanted to tell to someone I could trust werry p'ticlar, an' you've been a kind, true friend to the old man. My little Nell, the little lass as you've seen, wasn't born mine. A'most two year agone, a woman as was her mother, I s'pose, sell't her me in a lot o' old clo'es. She's been wi' me ever since, an' I love her like my own. She as seemed to be her mother was took to this place, dyin' from bein' run over by a conwayance. I hope the good Sisters helped her afore she died, an' that she didn't die bad."

Old Clo'es stops a while to get breath, and close by his side Nurse Mary stands, very pale, with her lips pressed together, and tears streaming fast from her eyes. She is listening, yes, drinking in greedily every word he says. But Old Clo'es' eyes are very dim, and he does not see her face.

"I've put by six pound i' the Savin's Bank for my little Nell," says Old Clo'es presently, "an' I want you to see as she has it, Nurse, if ye'll be so werry kind. Then there's two old books o' mine, one of 'em's called a 'Garding;' if ye'd give 'em to Lotty, she'll be pleased to have 'em for my sake!"

"Mister," cries Nurse Mary, throwing herself on her knees by the bedside, "I've somethin' to tell you. Listen!"

"Ay, Nurse, I'll listen!" says Old Clo'es.

"Mister, I do b'lieve it's your little Nell's own mother as is speakin' to you. I can't be quite sure, but I think it is!"

"Eh, what's that, Nurse?" says Old Clo'es gently.

"I'd a little lass; she was two year old, a pretty little lass as ever was. We come up from the country when her father died, to live in the city. But things got goin' from bad to worse. I got in a bad set, and they made me bad. I forgot most of the good I learnt in the Catholic school when I was a little un, an' what I couldn't forget, I tried my best to. But I always loved my little Polly; ay, better nor aught else, or I couldn't ha' done what I did for her sake!"

"Go on, Nurse; I'm list'nin'," says Old Clo'es.

"I was starvin' at last, an' so was she. It had come to that. I'd sold everything of my own. Then I seed an old man in the street one day with his bags, an' I see'd him werry kind to a little lass. I thought, 'He has a kind heart, has that old man.' An' the little lass I had by the hand was pinin' and cryin' for hunger. So I made my mind up. I gave her a drink to sleep her, an' I sold her to the ragman. Eh, it was hard—but I did it for her sake!"

"Go on, Nurse," says Old Clo'es.

"Well, then I went away. I couldn't bear to stay about the place. I threw away the shillin' I'd got for the child. I couldn't bear to buy me food wi' the price of her! By-and-bye I got work—enough to keep body and soul together; an' then——"

"An' then?" says Old Clo'es, eagerly.

"Then I tried to go back an' find the child. I wanted her. I couldn't live without her. I thought I'd steal her away, and no one 'ud know. I was her mother. I'd the best right to her. But I couldn't find her till one day when I saw a little lass like what mine might be picking up somethin' in the street. There was a carriage comin' past, and she was in its way, but she couldn't see it. I couldn't help but try to save her—she was so like my own. But I paid dear for it. I was run over in her place. They all thought I was dead, but I knew nothin' of it till I found myself here, and one of the good Sisters taking care of me. They said I was gettin' better then, but I was werry bad. When I got round, they sent me to the night-school to learn, and in the day I helped to nurse in the hospital. They've been werry good to me—body and soul. I told them of my trouble, and they're all prayin' that my little girl may be given me again."

"I b'lieve it's true," says Old Clo'es; "I b'lieve it's true! seems just as if my little Nell was your little lass. I should be werry glad if it was so."

"I can prove it, I think," Nurse Mary says; "but I'm almost afraid to, fear it shouldn't be my little lass after all! There was a mark on her arm as I made—a M for her name, so as I might p'r'aps know her again. Do you remember seein' it on her, mister?"

"Well, I can't say as I ever took p'tic'lar notice o' her arms," says Old Clo'es; "but I do mind Lotty sayin' as she'd a mark there—like a letter it was!"

"That's it; that's it! Then it is my little lass, after all!" says Mary Baker. "God has been very good to me in givin' her back to me."

"Eh, He *is* good!" says Old Clo'es; "but it's no use beginnin' to say it, or there's no knowin' where to stop. I feel I'm goin', but you're here all ready to take to my little lass. You'll know how, a deal better nor I should ha' done, bein' her mother."

"Ay, I'll take care o' the little one," says Mary Baker, wiping her eyes; "I'll do my best to bring her up as you'd ha' done, God helping me! She shall never forget her Dad as long as she lives—never. An' I don't know how to thank you for carin' for her an' lovin' her all this while. May Our Lord bless you for it!"

"Then I've nothin' more left on my mind now," says Old Clo'es. "Ain't it wonderful how things is cleared away for 'un? I can go werry peacefully when Our Lord wills, seein' my little Nell is all pervided for."

"She shall always be ' little Nell' with us," says Nurse Mary, tenderly. "Her own name was Mary, but she shall be called by the name you love."

"No," says Old Clo'es, in a gentle whisper; "I'm werry part'al to the name o' little Nelly, but Mary's a deal beautifuller. Why, little Nell's got Our Lady's own name! She'll be forced to keep *that*. An' my first little Nell is in heaven waitin' for me, so the name don't make such a great matter. Let it be Mary."

"It shall be just what you wish," says Nurse Mary.

"I feel I'm going soon," Old Clo'es whispers presently. "Could you send for 'em both—Lotty an' little Nell! I should like to say good-bye to 'em, an' to see my little lass an' her mother together afore I die."

So Lotty and little Nell come to the old

man's side, and Old Clo'es gives his little lovey into her mother's care, bidding them all come and join him some day in the home in which he hopes soon to be.

It is a very sad, yet a very bright parting.

The children's faces look very sad as they say good-bye for the last time; but on the old man's face there is only a happy calm.

He feels that it is all good and right.

By-and-bye it is all over, and the old man is laid away under the green sod. He has a few friends to pray for him, and a very warm place in their hearts.

Little Nell will never forget "Dad," however long her life may be. The great rag-bags that the old man carried and his leather purse are still kept by the child and her mother as a precious legacy and a loving memorial of

"OLD CLO'ES."

THE END.

R. WASHBOURNE, PRINTER, 18 PATERNOSTER ROW, LONDON.

"A glance at Mr. Washbourne's lists will always acquaint us where we may find light, diverting Catholic literature."—*Catholic Book News*, Jan., 1881.

# WASHBOURNE'S CATALOGUE

OF LIBRARY AND PRIZE BOOKS,
WITH NUMEROUS CRITICAL NOTICES,
AND LIST OF WORKS IMPORTED
FROM AMERICA. See page 20.
COMPLETE CATALOGUE SENT POST FREE.
18 *PATERNOSTER* ROW, LONDON.

Post Office Orders to be made payable to
Robert Washbourne, at the General Post Office.

Second Series of True Wayside Tales. By Lady Herbert. 3s., or separately :—
Moothoosawmy, or Natural Uprightness Supernaturally Rewarded; Saveriammal, or the Story of a Snake-bite and its Cure; Father Koblyowicz, or the Martyr to Sacramental Silence. 1s.
Emily; Nancy; the Efficacy of Prayer; and the White Necktie, a Story of First Communion. 1s.
The Two Cousins; The Result of a Mother's Prayers; and The Two School-boys. 1s.
Our Esther. By M. F. S., author of "Out in the Cold World." 2s. 6d.
The Gamekeeper's Little Son, and other Tales for Children. By the author of "Bobbie and Birdie." 2s. 6d.
Life of Rev. Fr. Hermann (Discalced Carmelite). From the French of the Abbé Charles Sylvani. By Mrs. Raymond-Barker. 8vo. cloth, 5s. 6d.; stronger bound, 6s. 6d.
Bobbie and Birdie; or, Our Lady's Picture. A Story for the very little ones. By Frances I. M. Kershaw. Fcap. 8vo., 2s. 6d.
Agnes Wilmott's History, and the Lessons it Taught. By M. A. Pennell, author of "Bertram Eldon," "Nellie Gordon," &c. 1s. 6d.
For Better, *not* For Worse. By Rev. Langton George Vere. [*In the press.*
Out in the Cold World. By M. F. S. (Mrs. Seamer), author of "Tom's Crucifix and other Tales," "Stories of the Lives of the Saints," &c. 3s. 6d.

**True Wayside Tales.** By Lady Herbert. 3s.; or may be had separately, in 5 volumes, cheap edition, in pretty binding, price 6d. each volume.
1. The Brigand Chief, and other Tales. 2. Now is the Accepted Time, and other Tales. 3. What a Child can do, and other Tales. 4. Sowing Wild Oats, and other Tales. 5. The Two Hosts, and other Tales.

"These tales are short, in good legible type, and evidently true."
—*Tablet.*

**Chats about the Commandments.** By M. F. Plues, author of "Chats about the Rosary." 3s.

"This book is written in a manner that would attract children, and we should think that it will be found a help by parents and teachers. . . . What you have written is very practical and true."—*Cardinal Manning.*

**Jack's Boy.** By M. F. S., author of "Tom's Crucifix, and other Tales," "Fluffy," etc. 3s. 6d.

"The author of 'Tom's Crucifix' is a favourite with many readers, old and young. There is a tender depth of feeling which runs through every page, and a simple earnestness and manifest truthfulness in the manner and style of the narration which renders her stories peculiarly attractive."—*Weekly Register.* "The more we have of such tales to move kind hearts, the better will it be for the children of the poor in our overgrown towns."—*The Month.*

**Bertram Eldon and how he found a home.** By M. A. Pennell, author of "Nellie Gordon." Cloth, 1s.

"Authors who will and can write little books like 'Bertram Eldon,' may hope to do much good thereby, for they are directly helping to inspire children with a love of the neglected poor, which will through after-life bear fruit in works of mercy."—*The Month.* "We can all learn a lesson from such a career as 'Bertie Eldon's.'"—*Catholic Times.*

**Walter Ferrers' School Days; or, Bellevue and its Owners.** By C. Pilley. 2s. Cheap edition, 1s.

"A family suffers a sudden reverse of fortune by the death of the father and the dishonesty of his agent. The Christian matron shows herself equal to the occasion, and her children find strength in her example, derive benefit from adversity, and struggle forward into happier times."—*The Month.* "A tale for the young. Its incidents are so arranged as to inculcate the practice of honesty and virtue, and a trust in the goodness of Providence. The juvenile mind will delight in it."—*Catholic Times.*

**The Golden Thought of Queen Beryl, and other Stories.** By Marie Cameron. 1s. 6d.; gilt edges, 2s., or may be had separately, cheap edition, in pretty binding, price 6d. each volume.
1. The Golden Thought, and The Brother's Grave.
2. The Rod that Bore Blossoms, and Patience and Impatience.

"Pleasantly written tales."—*Court Circular.*

**Clare's Sacrifice.** An impressive little tale, for First Communicants. By C. M. O'Hara. 6d.

**Nellie Gordon, the Factory Girl; or Lost and Saved.** By M. A. Pennell. 6d.

**Story of a Paper Knife.** By Henrica Frederic. 1s.

**The Siege and Conquest of Granada. Allah Akbar—God is Great.** From the Spanish. By Mariana Monteiro. Cloth Arabesque, 3s. 6d.

"A highly interesting story. The book is handsomely got up, and the illustrations, which are from the pencil of a sister of Miss Monteiro, add much to the beauty of the volume."—*Public Opinion.*

**Gathered Gems from Spanish Authors.** By Mariana Monteiro. 3s.

CONTENTS :—The Rosary Bell—The Blind Organist of Seville—The Last Baron of Fortcastells—The Miserere of the Mountains—Three Reminiscences—A Legend of Italy—The Gnomes of Monccay—The Passion Flower—Recollections of an Artistic Excursion—The Laurel Wreath—The Witches of Trasmoz.

"Genuine treasures of romance."—*Weekly Register.* "Particularly rich in pleasant stories of the purest morality."—*Irish Monthly.* "Of considerable beauty. . . . The high moral tone of it renders it far in advance of the majority of tales at the present day."—*Public Opinion.* "Much grace and freshness."—*University Magazine.*

**The Last Days of the Emperor Charles V., the Monk of the Monastery of Yuste.** An Historical Legend of the 16th century. From the Spanish, by Mariana Monteiro. 2s. 6d.

"An exceedingly interesting historical legend. It will amply repay perusal."—*Court Circular.* "A peculiar interest attaches to the tale."—*Weekly Register.* "It is well calculated to instruct and entertain the minds of young persons, since it is a tale of piety and also historical."—*Tablet.* "A very realistic picture of the character of Charles in monastic repose. We have read every page of the volume with much pleasure."—*Catholic Times.* "The whole narrative just the sort that might be put in the hands of a boy or girl under sixteen with advantage."—*Public Opinion.* "Well worthy of notice."—*The Month.*

**The Battle of Connemara.** By Kathleen O'Meara, author of "A Daughter of St. Dominick." 3s.

"Everything else is but a sketch, compared with the Irish scenes, which are written *con amore*, and though not very highly coloured, are faithful to life."—*Dublin Review.* "A charming story, charmingly told."—*Irish Monthly.* "A book which has interested us; in which others, we doubt not, will take much interest."—*Tablet.* "The sketch of the Holy Mass in the miserable thatched building is one of the most effective bits of description we have seen; and this portrayal of peasant life, privation, and faith is too accurate to be questioned."—*Catholic Times.* "This interesting tale."—*The Month.*

The Dark Shadow. A Tale. 3s.

Industry and Laziness. By Franz Hoffman. From the German, by James King. 12mo., 3s.

"This is a capital story for boys. We can assure youthful readers that they will find much to attract them in this adventurous story."—*Weekly Register.* "The moral is excellent, the interest of the story well sustained."—*Tablet.* "A good, moral story."—*Court Circular.* "Any book that tries to save boys and young men from copying the example of John Collins deserves to be encouraged, especially when it is so very readably written and printed as the present tale."—*Irish Monthly.*

The Fairy Ching; or the Chinese Fairies' Visit to England. By Henrica Frederic. Handsomely bound in cloth extra, 1s., gilt edges 1s. 6d.

My Golden Days. By M. F. S. 12mo., 2s. 6d., or in 3 vols., 1s. each; gilt, 1s. 6d.
 The One Ghost of my Life, Willie's Escape, &c.
 The Captain's Monkey, &c.
 Great Uncle Hugh, Long Dresses, &c.

"They are playfully descriptive of the little ways and experience of young people, and are well suited for reading aloud in a family circle of juveniles."—*The Month.* "A series of short tales for children, by the delightful author of 'Fluffy' and a score of other charming books for the young."—*Weekly Register.* "Capital tales for children, nicely told, printed in large type on good paper and neatly bound."—*The Bookseller.* "Feelings run through them like a stream through flowers, and pretty morals peep out as the reader travels along."—*Catholic Times.* "This is the latest of the long catalogue of bright and edifying books of short stories for which our young people have to thank M. F. S."—*Irish Monthly.*

From Sunrise to Sunset. A Catholic Tale. 3s. 6d.

"A story for young readers, with a distinctly religious tendency, well written and interesting."—*The Bookseller.* "A pleasing tale, of which some of the incidents take place in the Grisons of Switzerland. There is a good power of description of scenery, in very clear grammatical language. In fact, the purity of style of L. B. is quite an example to the average novel writer."—*Public Opinion.* "A lively, chatty, pleasant little novel, which can do no harm to any one, and may afford amusement to many young persons."—*Tablet.*

The Two Friends; or, Marie's Self-denial. By Madame d'Arras (*Née* Lechmere). 1s.; gilt, 1s. 6d.

"A little French tale, in the crisis of which the good Empress Eugénie plays a conspicuous part."—*Weekly Register.*

Andersen's Sketches of Life in Iceland. Translated by Myfanwy Fenton. 2s.; cheaper edition, 1s. 6d.

"In the one case they are simply pretty tales; in the other curious illustrations of the survival to our own time of thought and manners familiar to every reader of the Sagas."—*Graphic.* "Ever welcome additions to the literary flora of a primitive and little-known country, such as Iceland must still be deemed. The Princess of Wales has been pleased to accept this unpretentious little story-book, written in the high latitudes where legends flourish abundantly."—*Public Opinion.* " Told with simple eloquence. A happy mean of refreshing simplicity which every reader must enjoy."—*Catholic Times.* " The style is fresh and simple, and the little volume is altogether very attractive."—*Weekly Register.*

Rest, on the Cross. By E. L. Hervey. Author of " The Feasts of Camelot," &c. 12mo., 3s. 6d.

" This is a heart-thrilling story of many trials and much anguish endured by the heroine. Rest comes to her, where alone it can come to all. The little tale is powerfully and vividly told."—*Weekly Register.* " Mrs. Hervey has shown a rare talent in the relation of moral tales calculated to fascinate and impress younger readers."—*Somerset County Gazette.* " An interesting and well-written religious story for young people."—*The Bookseller.* " An emotional and gushing little novelette."—*Church Times.* " It is impossible for us to know how far the events and situations are real, and how far imaginary ; but if real, they are well related, and if imaginary, they are well conceived."—*Tablet.* " It is written in the gentlest spirit of charity."—*Athenæum.*

The Feasts of Camelot, with the Tales that were told there. By Eleanora Louisa Hervey. 3s. 6d. ; or separately, Christmas, 1s. 6d.; Whitsuntide, 1s. 6d.

" This is really a very charming collection of tales, told as is evident from the title, by the Knights of the Round Table, at the Court of King Arthur. It is good for children and for grown up people too, to read these stories of knightly courtesy and adventure and of pure and healthy romance, and they have never been written in a more attractive style than by Mrs. Hervey in this little volume."—*Tablet.* " This is a very charming story book."—*Weekly Register.* " Mrs. Hervey brings the great legendary hero within the reach of children, but the stories are quite sufficiently well told to deserve the perusal of more critical readers."—*The Month.* " These tales are well constructed, and not one of them is destitute of interest."—*Catholic Times.* Full of chivalry and knightly deeds, not unmixed with touches of quaint humour."—*Court Journal.* " A graceful and pleasing collection of stories."—*Daily News.* " There is a high purpose in this charming book, one which is steadily pursued—it is the setting forth of the true meaning of chivalry."—*Morning Post.*

Stories from many Lands. By E. L. Hervey. 3s. 6d.

" Very well and, above all, very briefly told. The stories are short and varied. The Godmother's Anecdotes are very good stories."—*Saturday Review.* " A great number of short Stories and Anecdotes of a good moral tone."—*Tablet.* " A delightful fairy Godmother is this, who promises to rival the famous Princess Scheherezade as a story-teller."—*Weekly Register.* " Suitable for boys and girls of ten or twelve years, and is capable of teaching them not a few wholesome truths in an agreeable but really impressive manner."—*Illustrated London News.* " A charming collection of tales, illustrating some great truths."—*Church Times*. "With a few exceptions each story has 'some heart of meaning in it,' and tends to kindle in the mind all that is good and noble."—*Windsor Gazette*. "A collection of short stories, anecdotes, and apologues on various topics, delightfully told."—*Athenæum*.

**A Daughter of St. Dominic.** By Grace Ramsay (Kathleen O'Meara). 1s.; stronger bound, 1s. 6d.; cloth extra, 2s.

"A beautiful little work. The narrative is highly interesting."—*Dublin Review*. "It is full of courage and faith and Catholic heroism."—*Universe*. "A beautiful picture of the wonders effected by ubiquitous charity, and still more by fervent prayer."—*Tablet*.

**Bessy; or the Fatal Consequence of Telling Lies.** 1s.; stronger bound, 1s. 6d.; gilt, 2s.

"This is a very good tale to put into the hands of young servants."—*Tablet*. "The moral teaching is of course thoroughly Catholic, and conveyed in a form extremely interesting."—*Weekly Register*.

**Kainer; or, the Usurer's Doom.** By the Author of "Industry and Laziness." 1s., gilt edges, 1s. 6d.

"A very tastefully printed book, and the translation is clear and tasteful—well done, in fact."—*Irish Monthly*.

**Tom's Crucifix, and other Tales.** By M. F. S. 3s. 6d.; or separately, 1s. each, or 1s. 6d. gilt.

Tom's Crucifix, and Pat's Rosary.
Good for Evil, and Joe Ryan's Repentance.
The Old Prayer Book, and Charlie Pearson's Medal.
Catherine's Promise, and Norah's Temptation.
Annie's First Prayer, and Only a Picture.

"Simple stories for the use of teachers of Christian doctrine."—*Universe*. "This is a volume of short, plain, and simple stories, written with the view of illustrating the Catholic religion practically by putting Catholic practices in an interesting light before the mental eyes of children. The whole of the tales in the volume before us are exceedingly well written."—*Weekly Register*.

**Fluffy. A Tale for Boys.** By M. F. S., author of "Tom's Crucifix and other Tales." 3s. 6d.

"A charming little story. The narrative is as wholesome through out as a breath of fresh air, and as beautiful in the spirit of it as a beam of moonlight."—*Weekly Register*. "The tale is well told, We cannot help feeling an interest in the fortunes of Fluffy."—*Tablet*.

**The Three Wishes. A Tale.** By M. F. S. 2s. 6d. Cheaper edition, 1s. 6d.

"A pretty neatly told story for girls. There is much quiet pathos in it and a warm Catholic spirit."—*The Month.* "We are glad to welcome this addition to the story-books for which the author is already favourably known."—*United Irishman.* "The tale is singularly interesting. The story of Gertrude with her gratified wish has about it all the interest of a romance, and will, no doubt, find especial favour."—*Weekly Register.* "Like everything which M. F. S. writes, the book is full of interest."—*Tablet.* The chief heroine is a striking model of what a young woman ought to be, and may become, if animated by sincere desire."—*Catholic Times.*

**Catherine Hamilton.** By M. F. S. 2s. 6d. ; gilt, 3s.

"We have no doubt this will prove a very attractive book to the little folks, and would be glad to see it widely circulated."—*Catholic World.* "A short, simple, and well-told story, illustrative of the power of grace to correct bad temper in a wayward girl."—*Weekly Register.* "We are very much pleased with this little book."—*Tablet.*

**Catherine grown Older.** By M. F. S. 2s. 6d. ; gilt 3s.

"Those who are familiar with the history of Catherine in her wayward childhood will welcome with no little satisfaction this sequel to her story from the hand of the same charming writer. There is a simplicity about the style and an earnest tenderness in the manner of the narrative which renders it singularly impressive."—*Weekly Register.* "Catherine's character will delight English children."—*Tablet.*

**The Angels and the Sacraments.**—Stories for my Children. 1s. ; gilt, 1s. 6d.

**Simple Tales.** Square 16mo., cloth antique, 2s. 6d.

"Contains five pretty stories of a true Catholic tone, interspersed with some short pieces of poetry. . . Are very affecting, and told in such a way as to engage the attention of any child."—*Register.* "This is a little book which we can recommend with great confidence. The tales are simple, beautiful, and pathetic."—*Catholic Opinion.* "It belongs to a class of books of which the want is generally much felt by Catholic parents."—*Dublin Review.* "Beautifully written. 'Little Terence' is a gem of a Tale."—*Tablet.*

**Terry O'Flinn.** By the Very Rev. Dr. Tandy. Fcap. 8vo. 1s. ; stronger bound, 1s. 6d. ; gilt, 2s.

"The writer possesses considerable literary power."—*Register.* "A most singular production."—*Universe.* "An unpretending yet a very touching story."—*Waterford News.* "Excellent indeed is the idea of embodying into a story the belief that there is ever beside us a guardian angel who reads the thoughts of our hearts and strives to turn us to good."—*Catholic World.* "The idea is well sustained throughout."—*Church Times.*

**The Adventures of a Protestant in Search of a Religion**: being the Story of a late Student of Divinity at Bunyan Baptist College ; a Nonconformist Minister, who seceded to the Catholic Church. By Iota. 3s. 6d. ; cheap edition, 2s.

"Will well repay its perusal."—*Universe.* "This precious volume."—*Baptist.* "No one will deny 'Iota' the merit of entire originality."—*Civilian.* "A valuable addition to every Catholic library." *Tablet.* "There is much cleverness in it."—*Nonconformist.* "Malicious and wicked."—*English Independent.* "An admirable and amusing, yet truthful and genuinely sparkling work. The characters are from life."—*Catholic Opinion.*

The Village Lily. Fcap. 8vo. 1s.; gilt, 1s. 6d.

"Charming little story."—*Weekly Register.*

Fairy Tales for Little Children. By Madeleine Howley Meehan. 6d.; cloth, 1s. and 1s. 6d.; gilt, 2s.

"Full of imagination and dreams, and at the same time with excellent point and practical aim, within the reach of the intelligence of infants."—*Universe.* "Pleasing, simple stories, combining instruction with amusement."—*Register.* A pretty little book to give to imaginative young ones."—*Tablet.*

Rosalie; or, the Memoirs of a French Child. Written by herself. 1s.; stronger bound, 1s. 6d.; gilt, 2s.

'It is prettily told, and in a natural manner. The account of Rosalie's illness and First Communion is very well related. We can recommend the book for the reading of children."—*Tablet.* "The tenth chapter is beautiful."—*Universe.* "The lessons inculcated tend to improve the youthful mind. We cannot too strongly recommend the book."—*Waterford News.* "This is one of those nicely written stories for children which we now and then come across."—*Catholic World.* "Charmingly written."—*Church Herald.*

The Story of Marie and other Tales. 2s. 6d.; gilt, 3s.

"A very nice little collection of stories, thoroughly Catholic in their teaching."—*Tablet.* "A series of short pretty stories, told with much simplicity."—*Universe.* "A number of short pretty stories, replete with religious teaching, told in simple language."—*Weekly Register.*

The Mission Cross. An Abstinence Tale. By Mrs. Bartle Teeling, author of "Roman Violets," and "The Violet Sellers—a Drama." 2s.

Sir Ælfric and other Tales. By the Rev. G. Bampfield. 18mo. 6d.; cloth, 1s.; gilt, 1s. 6d.

The Last of the Catholic O'Malleys. A Tale. By M. Taunton. cloth, 1s. 6d.; stronger bound, 2s.

"A sad and stirring tale, simply written, and sure to secure for itself readers."—*Tablet.* "Deeply interesting. It is well adapted for parochial and school libraries."—*Weekly Register.* "A very pleasing tale."—*The Month.* "Simply and naturally told."—*Freeman's Journal.*

My Lady at Last. A Tale. By M. Taunton, author of "The Last of the Catholic O'Malleys." 5s.

Killed at Sedan. A Novel. By Samuel Richardson, A.B., B.L., of the Middle Temple. 10s. 6d.

Eagle and Dove. From the French of Zénaïde Fleuriot, by Emily Bowles. 5s.; cheaper, 2s. 6d.

"We recommend our readers to peruse this well-written story."—*Register*. "One of the very best stories we have ever dipped into."—*Church Times*. "Admirable in tone and purpose."—*Church Herald*. "A real gain. It possesses merits far above the pretty fictions got up by English writers."—*Dublin Review*. "There is an air of truth and sobriety about this little volume, nor is there any attempt at sensation."—*Tablet*.

Legends of the 13th Century. By the Rev. Henry Collins. 3s.; or in 3 vols., 1s. 6d. each.

"A casket of jewels. Most fascinating as legends and none the less profitable for example, consolation, and encouragement."—*Weekly Register*. "The legends are full of deep spiritual teaching, and they are almost all authenticated."—*Tablet*. "Well translated and beautifully got up."—*The Month*. "Full of heavenly wisdom,"—*Catholic Opinion*. "The volume reminds us forcibly of Rodriguez's 'Christian Perfection.'"—*Dublin Review*.

Little Books of St. Nicholas. Tales for Children. By Rev. F. Drew. 1s. each.

1. Oremus; 2. Dominus Vobiscum; 3. Pater Noster; 4. Per Jesum Christum; 5. Veni Creator; 6. Credo; 7. Ave Maria; 8. Ora pro nobis; 9. Corpus Christi; 10. Dei Genitrix; 11. Requiem; 12. Miserere; 13. Deo Gratias; 14. Guardian Angel. [Numbers 1 to 7 are ready.]

Keighley Hall and other Tales. By E. King. Gilt, 2s.

"The religious teaching is very good, and stamps the work as being that of a loyal member of the one true Church."—*Tablet*. "The Tales are Catholic to the backbone."—*Weekly Register*. "Interesting and well-written stories."—*Westminster Gazette*. "Very interesting as stories."—*Church News*. "Full of devotion and piety."—*Northern Press*.

Chats about the Rosary; or, Aunt Margaret's Little Neighbours. By Miss Plues. Fcap. 8vo. 3s.

"There is scarcely any devotion so calculated as the Rosary to keep up a taste for piety in little children, and we must be grateful for any help in applying its lessons to the daily life of those who already love it in their unconscious tribute to its value and beauty."—*Month*. "We do not know of a better book for reading aloud to children, it will teach them to understand and to love the Rosary."—*Tablet*. Illustrative of each of the mysteries, and connecting each with the practice of some particular virtue."—*Catholic Opinion*. "This pretty book carries out a very good idea, much wanted, to impress upon people who do not read much the vivid picture or story of each mystery of the Rosary."—*Dublin Review*.

**The Rose of Venice.** A Tale, relating to the Council of Ten in the Venetian Republic. By S. Christopher. Crown 8vo., 5s.

"A very interesting and well-told story."—*The Month.*

**Margarethe Verflassen.** Translated from the German by Mrs. Smith Sligo. 1s. 6d. and 3s.; gilt, 3s. 6d.

"A portrait of a very holy and noble soul, whose life was passed in constant practical acts of the love of God."—*Weekly Register.* "It is the picture of a true woman's life, well fitted up with the practice of ascetic devotion and loving unwearied activity about all the works of mercy."—*Tablet.* "Those who may wish to know something about Convent life will find it faithfully pourtrayed in every important particular in the volume before us. We cordially commend it to our readers."—*Northern Star.*

**Ned Rusheen.** By Sister M. F. Clare. 5s.

**The Prussian Spy.** A Novel. By V. Valmont. 4s.

**Sir Thomas Maxwell and his Ward.** By Miss Bridges. Fcap. 8vo. 1s.

**Adolphus; or, the Good Son.** 18mo. gilt, 6d.

**Nicholas; or, the Reward of a Good Action.** 6d.

**The Lost Children of Mount St. Bernard.** Gilt, 6d.

**The Baker's Boy; or, the Results of Industry.** 6d.

**A Broken Chain.** 18mo. gilt, 6d.

**Tales and Sketches.** By Charles Fleet. 8vo. 3s. 6d.

**Cardinal Wolsey; or the Abbot of St. Cuthbert's.** By Agnes Stewart. 6s. 6d.

**Sir Thomas More.** By the same author. 10s. 6d.

**The Yorkshire Plot.** By the same author. 6s. 6d.

**Bishop Fisher.** By the same author. 7s. 6d.

**Limerick Veteran.** By the same author. 4s. 6d.

**Life in the Cloister.** By the same author. 3s. 6d.

**Festival Tales.** By J. F. Waller. 3s. 6d.

**Rupert Aubray.** By the Rev. T. J. Potter. 3s.

**Percy Grange.** By the same author. 3s.

**Farleyes of Farleye.** By the same author. 2s. 6d.

**Sir Humphrey's Trial.** By the same author. 2s. 6d.

**The Victims of the Mamertine.** Scenes from the Early Church. By Rev. A. J. O'Reilly. D.D. 5s.

**The Catholic "Pilgrim's Progress"**—The Journey of Sophia and Eulalie to the Palace of True Happiness. Translated by the Rev. Father Bradbury, Mount St. Bernard's. 1s. 6d., better bound, 3s. 6d.

"The book is essentially suited to women, and especially to those who purpose devoting themselves to the hidden life of sanctity. It will prove, however, a useful gift to many young ladies whose lot is in the world."—*Weekly Register.* "This mode of teaching imparts an extraordinary degree of vividness and reality."—*Church Review.* "Unquestionably the book is one that for a certain class of minds will have a great charm."—*The Scotsman.* "No one can weary with the perusal, and most people will enjoy it very much."—*Tablet.*

**Diary of a Confessor of the Faith.** 12mo., 1s.

**Recollections of the Reign of Terror.** By the Abbé Dumesnil. 2s. 6d.

**Tim O'Halloran's Choice; or, From Killarney to New York.** By Sister M. F. Clare. 3s. 6d.

**The Silver Teapot.** By Elizabeth King. 18mo., 4d.

**The First Christmas for our dear little ones.** By Miss Mulholland. 15 Illustrations, 4to. 6s.

**Legends of the Saints.** By M. F. S., author of "Stories of the Saints." Square 16mo., 3s. 6d.

"A pretty little book, couched in studiously simple language."—*Church Times.* "A number of short legends, told in simple language for young readers by one who has already given us two charming volumes of 'Stories of the Saints.'"—*Tablet.* "Here we have more than fifty tales, told with singular taste, and ranging over a vast geographical area. Not one of them will be passed over by the reader."—*Catholic Times.* "A delightful boon for youthful readers."—*Weekly Register.* "It is got up in the most attractive as well as substantial style as regards binding, paper, and typography, while the simple and beautiful legends are told in a graceful and flowing manner, which cannot fail to rivet the attention and interest of the youthful reader."—*United Irishman.*

**Stories of the Saints.** By M. F. S. 1st Series, 3s. 6d., gilt, 4s. 6d. 2nd Series, 3s. 6d., gilt, 4s. 6d. 3rd Series, 3s. 6d. 4th Series, 3s. 6d. 5th Series, 3s. 6d.

"As lovely a little book as we have seen for many a day."—*Weekly Register.* "Interesting not only for children but for persons of every age and degree."—*Tablet.* "A great desideratum. Very pleasantly written."—*The Month.* "A very attractive volume. A delightful book."—*Union Review.* "Admirably adapted for reading aloud to children, or for their own private reading."—*Catholic Opinion.* "Being full of anecdotes, they are especially attractive."—*Church Herald.* "Well selected."—*Dublin Review.*

**Stories of Holy Lives.** By M. F. S. Fcp. 8vo., 3s. 6d.

"The stories seem well put together."—*The Month.* "It sets before us clearly and in simple language the most striking features in the character and history of many whose very names are dear to the hearts of Catholics."—*Tablet.*

**Stories of Martyr Priests.** By M. F. S. 12mo., 3s. 6d.

"The stories are written with the utmost simplicity, and with such an earnest air of reality about every page that the youthful reader may forget that he has a book in his hand, and can believe that he is 'listening to a story.'"—*Weekly Register.* "It has been the task of the writer, while adhering strictly to historical facts, to present the lives of these Christian heroes in a pleasing and attractive form, so that, while laying before the youthful minds deeds as thrilling as any to be found in the pages of romance, a chapter in her history is laid open which is at once the glory and the shame of England."—*United Irishman.* "Short memoirs well written and which cannot fail to attract not only 'the Catholic Boys of England,' to whom the book is dedicated, but also all the men and women of England to whom the Catholic faith is dear."—*Tablet.* "Sad stories of over thirty Priests who perished for conscience sake."—*Catholic Times.* "No lives of great men can depict so glorious a picture as these Stories of Martyred Priests, and we trust they will be read far and wide."—*Dublin Review.*

**The Story of the Life of St. Paul.** By M. F. S., author of "Legends of the Saints," &c. 2s. 6d. and 1s. 6d.

"A most attractive theme for the prolific pen of the author of 'Tom's Crucifix and other Tales.'"—*Weekly Register.* "The author knew instinctively how to present the incidents most effectively, and has made the most of them."—*Catholic Times.*

**Bible Stories from the Old Testament.** Twelve Stories of the Jewish Church, to interest the young in the fortunes of God's ancient Church, by throwing the Scripture narrative into a slightly different form. By Charles Walker. Cloth, extra, 2s. 6d. Cheaper edition, 1s. 6d.

CONTENTS:—The Sacrifice of Abel.—The Ship of Safety.—The City of Confusion.—Melchisedech, King of Salem.—The Sabbath Breaker.—Achan.—The Child Prophet of Silo.—The Building of the Temple.—The Altar at Beth-El.—The Repentance of Nineve.—The Furnace of Babylon.—The Prophecy of Malachias.

**Albertus Magnus**: his Life and Scholastic Labours. From original Documents. By Professor Sighart. Translated by Rev. Fr. T. A. Dixon, O.P. With a Portrait. 8vo., 10s. 6d.; cheap edition, 5s.

"A translation of Dr. Sighart's 'Albertus Magnus' will be welcome in many quarters. The volume is admirably printed and beautifully got up, and the frontispiece is a valuable engraving of B. Albert's portrait after Fiesole."—*Dublin Review.* " Albert the Great is not well known . . . yet he is one of those pioneers of inductive philosophy whom our modern men of science cannot without black ingratitude forget. His memory should be dear not only to those who value the sanctity of life, but to those also who try, as he did, to wrest from nature the reason of her doings."—*The Month.* " The volume is a large one, as befits the subject, and it carries the reader through most of the scenes of Albert's life with a graphic power . . . We recommend this book as worthy a place in every library."—*Catholic Times.* " The fullest record that has ever been penned of one of the grandest luminaries in the history of the Church."—*Weekly Register.* " The book is extremely interesting, full of information, and displays great power of research and critical judgment. . . . The volume is eminently worth perusal."—*Tablet.* " One of the most interesting religious biographies recently issued from the Catholic press."—*Irish Monthly.*

Life of St. Wenefred, Virgin Martyr and Abbess, Patroness of North Wales and Shrewsbury. By Rev. T. Meyrick, M.A. With Frontispiece, 2s.

Lives of the Saints for every Day in the Year. Beautifully printed on thick toned paper, within borders from ancient sources. Cloth gilt, gilt edges, 4to. 25s.

Lives of the First Religious of the Visitation of Holy Mary. By Mother Frances Magdalen de Chaugy. 2 vols., 10s. :—or separately :—

Life of Mother Marie Jacqueline Favre, Mother Jeanne Charlotte de Bréchard, Mother Peronne Marie de Châtel, Mother Claude Agnes Joli de la Roche. 6s.

Life of Sister Claude Simplicienne Fardel, Sister Marie Aimée de Chantal, Sister Françoise Gabrielle Bally, Sister Marie Denise de Martignat, Sister Anne Jacqueline Coste, Sister Marie Péronne Pernet, Sister Marie Séraphique de Chamflours. 6s.

S. Vincent Ferrer, his Life, Spiritual Teaching, and practical Devotion. By Fr. Pradel. Translated by Rev. Fr. Dixon, O.P. With Photograph, 5s.

Life of S. Bernardine of Siena. With a portrait, 5s.

Life of S. Philip Benizi. With a portrait, 5s.

Life of S. Veronica Giuliani, and Blessed Battista Varani. With a portrait, 5s.

Life of S. John of God. With a portrait, 5s.

The Lives of the Early Popes. By Rev. Thomas Meyrick, M.A., 2 vols., 8vo. St. Peter to St. Silvester, 4s. 6d. From the time of Constantine to Charlemagne, 5s. 6d.

Life of B. Giovanni Colombini. By Feo Belcari. Translated from the editions of 1541 and 1832. With a Photograph. Cr. 8vo. 3s. 6d.

Life of Sister Mary Frances of the Five Wounds. From the Italian. By Rev. D. Ferris. 2s. 6d.

Sketch of the Life and Letters of the Countess Adelstan. By E. A. M., author of "Rosalie, or the Memoirs of a French Child," "Life of Paul Seigneret," &c. 1s.; better bound, 2s. 6d.

"The great interest of the book, even above the story of the conversion of her husband, is the question of education. The essay on the bringing up of children and the comparative merits and demerits of Convent and home education, is well worth the careful study both of parents and those entrusted with the task of instruction."—*The Month.* "Her judgments are always wise."—*Catholic Opinion.* "We can safely recommend this excellent little biographical sketch. It offers no exciting interest, but it is calculated to edify all."—*Tablet.*

Life of Paul Seigneret, Seminarist of Saint-Sulpice. 6d.; cloth, 1s.; better bound, 1s. 6d.; gilt, 2s.

"An affecting and well-told narrative. . . It will be a great favourite, especially with our pure-minded, high-spirited young people."—*Universe.* "We commend it to parents with sons under their care, and especially do we recommend it to those who are charged with the education and training of our Catholic youth."—*Register.*

Inner Life of Père Lacordaire. By Père Chocarne. Translated by Augusta Theodosia Drane. 6s. 6d.

Life of Sister Mary Cherubina Clare of S. Francis. With Preface by Lady Herbert, and Photograph, 3s. 6d.

Life and Letters of Sir Thomas More. By A. M. Stewart. Illustrated, 8vo., 10s. 6d.; gilt, 11s 6d.

Life of Gregory Lopez, the Hermit. By Canon Doyle O.S.B. With a Photograph. 12mo., 3s. 6d.

St. Angela Merici. Her Life, her Virtues, and her Institute. 12mo., 3s.

Life of St. Columba, &c. By M. F. Cusack. 8vo., 6s.

Recollections of Cardinal Wiseman, &c. By M. J. Arnold. 2s. 6d.

Prince and Saviour. A Life of Christ for the Young. By Rosa Mulholland. 1s. 6d. Cheap edition, 6d.

Life and Miracles of St. Benedict. From St. Gregory the Great, by Rev. Dom E. J. Luck. 4to., 10s. 6d. With 52 large Photographs, 31s. 6d. Small Edition, fcap. 8vo., 2s.; stronger bound, 2s. 6d.

Life of St. Boniface. By Mrs. Hope. 6s.

Life of Fr. Benvenuto Bambozzi, O.M.C., of the Conventual Friars Minor. Translated from the Italian of Fr. Nicholas Treggiari, D.D. 5s.

Life of the Ven. Anna Maria Taigi. From the French of Calixte, by A. V. Smith Sligo. 2s. 6d. better bound, 5s.

Venerable Mary Christina of Savoy. 6d.

Life of Father Mathew. By Sister Mary Francis Clare. 2s. 6d.

Life of St. Patrick. 12mo. 1s.; 8vo., 6s., gilt, 10s.

Life of St. Bridget, and of other Saints of Ireland. 1s.

The Life of Our Lord. With Introduction by Dr. Husenbeth. Illustrated. 5s.

Life, Passion, Death, and Resurrection of Our Blessed Lord. Translated from Ribadeneira. 1s.

Life of S. Edmund of Canterbury. 1s. and 1s. 6d.

Life of St. Francis of Assisi. From St. Bonaventure. By Miss Lockhart. With Photograph, 3s. 6d.

Life of St. German. 3s. 6d.

Life of Cardinal Wiseman. 1s.; cloth, 1s. 6d.

Life of Count de Montalembert. By G. White. 6d.

Life of Mgr. Weedall. By Dr. Husenbeth. 5s.

Pius IX. By J. F. Maguire. 6s.

Pius IX. From his Birth to his Death. By G. White. 6d.

Life of the Ever-Blessed Virgin. 1s.

Our Blessed Lady of Lourdes: a Faithful Narrative of the Apparitions of the Blessed Virgin. By F. C. Husenbeth, D.D. 18mo. 6d.; cloth, 1s.; with Novena, 1s.; cloth, 1s. 6d. Novena, separately, 4d.; Litany, 1d., or 6s. per 100. Medal, 1d.

A Month at Lourdes and its Neighbourhood in the Summer of 1877. By Hugh Caraher. Two Illustrations, 2s.

The History of the Blessed Virgin. By Orsini. Translated by Dr. Husenbeth. Illustrated, 3s. 6d.

Devotion to Our Lady in North America. By the Rev. Xavier Donald Macleod. 8vo. 5s.

"The work of an author than whom few more gifted writers have ever appeared among us. It is not merely a religious work, but it has all the charms of an entertaining book of travels. We can hardly find words to express our high admiration of it."—*Weekly Register.*

Life of the Ven. Elizabeth Canori Mora. From the Italian, with Preface by Lady Herbert, and Photograph. 3s. 6d.

The History of the Italian Revolution. The Revolution of the Barricades. (1796—1849.) By the Chevalier O'Clery, M.P., K.S.G. 8vo. 7s. 6d.; cheap edition, 3s. 6d.

"The volume is ably written, and by a man who is acquainted with the subject about which he writes."—*Athenæum.* "Well-written, and contains many passages that are marked by candour and amiability."—*Guardian.* "Mr. O'Clery's graphic and truthful narrative. ... Written in an easy flowing style, the volume is by no means heavy reading."—*Pilot.* "It was a happy thought on the part of Mr. O'Clery to conceive the possibility of contributing something towards the removal of the existing ignorance; and it was better still to have girded himself up to the task of giving execution to his thought in the very able and satisfactory manner in which he has done his work."—*The Month.* "The author grasps the whole subject of the Revolution with a master mind.... From the first page to the last it is of absorbing interest."—*Catholic Times.* "Written with the calmness of the historian, yet with something of the energy of faith, this book cannot fail to be most interesting to Catholics. The style is easy and enjoyable."—*Tablet.* "In every line of the book we find a vigour and freshness of mind, combined with a maturity of judgment on the great question at issue."—*Wexford People.*

Two Years in the Pontifical Zouaves. By Joseph Powel, Z.P. With 4 Engravings. 8vo. 3s. 6d.

"It affords us much pleasure, and deserves the notice of the Catholic public."—*Tablet.* "Familiar names meet the eye on every pages and as few Catholic circles in either country have not had a friend or relative at one time or another serving in the Pontifical Zouaves, the history of the formation of the corps, of the gallant youths, their sufferings, and their troubles, will be valued as something more than a contribution to modern Roman history."—*Freeman's Journal.*

**Rome and her Captors.** Letters collected and edited by Count Henri d'Ideville, and translated by F. R. Wegg-Prosser. Cr. 8vo. 4s.

"The letters describe the attempted capture of Rome by Garibaldi; and the tissue of events which brought about in 1870 the seizure of Rome by Victor Emanuel."—*Dublin Review.* "A series of letters graphically depicting the course of political events in Italy, and showing in its true light the dishonesty of the Piedmontese government, the intrigues of Prussia, and the ill-treatment to which the Pope has been subjected. We most cordially recommend the volume to our readers."—*Church Herald.* "One of the most opportune contributions that could be made to popular literature."—*Cork Examiner.* "We have read the book carefully, and have found it full of interest."—*Catholic Opinion.*

**Personal Recollections of Rome.** By W. J. Jacob, Esq., late of the Pontifical Zouaves. 8vo. 1s. 6d.

"An interesting description of the Eternal City . . . The value of the Pamphlet is enhanced by a catena of authorities on the Temporal Power."—*Tablet.* "All will read it with pleasure, and many to their profit."—*Weekly Register.* "We cordially recommend an attentive perusal of Mr. Jacob's book."—*Nation.*

**To Rome and Back.** Fly-leaves from a Flying Tour. Edited by W. H. Anderdon, S.J. 12mo., 2s.

'Graphic and vigorous sketches. As Father Anderdon says, Truly they have their special interest, by reason of date no less than of place and scene. 'To Rome and Back' refers to Rome and back at the time of the Papal Jubilee. It is as beautiful a celebration of that memorable event as has anywhere appeared."—*Weekly Register.* "We note in the Authoress a power of condensing a description in a bold and striking metaphor. There is all a woman's quickness and keenness of perception, and a power of sympathy with the noble, the beautiful, and the true."—*The Month.* "A charming book. . . . Besides pleasant description, there is evidence of much thought in parts of the book."—*Dublin Review.*

**The First Apostles of Europe.** The 2nd Edition of "The Conversion of the Teutonic Race." By Mrs. Hope. 2 vols. crown 8vo. 10s.

"Mrs. Hope has quite grasped the general character of the Teutonic nations and their true position with regard to Rome and the world in general. . . It is a great thing to find a writer of a book of this class so clearly grasping and so boldly setting forth truths, which familiar as they are to scholars, are still utterly unknown—or worse than unknown, utterly misconceived—by most of the writers of our smaller literature."—*Saturday Review.* "A brilliant and compact history of the Germans, Franks, and the various tribes of the former Jutes, Angles, and Saxons, who jointly formed the Anglo-Saxon, or, more correctly, English people. . . . Many of the episodes and notices of the Apostolic Missionaries, as well as the general story, are very happily and gracefully conveyed.'—*Northern Star.* "This is a real addition to our Catholic literature."—*Tablet.* "In the first place it is good in itself, possessing considerable literary merit ; then it fills up a blank, which has never yet been occupied, to the generality of readers, and lastly and beyond all, it forms one of the few Catholic books brought out in this country which are not translations or adaptations from across the Channel. It is a growth of individual intellectual labour, fed from original sources, and fused by the polish of a cultivated and discerning mind."—*Dublin Review.* " Mrs. Hope's historical works are always valuable."—*Weekly Register.* "A very valuable work ... Mrs. Hope has compiled an original history, which gives constant evidence of great erudition, and sound historical judgment.' —*The Month.* "This is a most taking book : it is solid history and romance in one."—*Catholic Opinion.* " It is carefully, and in many parts beautifully written, and the account of the Irish monks is most instructive and interesting."—*Universe.*

BY ARTHUR AND T. W. M. MARSHALL.

Comedy of Convocation in the English Church. Edited by Archdeacon Chasuble, D.D. 2s. 6d.

The Oxford Undergraduate of Twenty Years Ago : his Religion, his Studies, his Antics. By a Bachelor of Arts. 2s. 6d. ; cloth, 3s. 6d.

" The writing is full of brilliancy and point."—*Tablet.* " It will deservedly attract attention, not only by the briskness and liveliness of its style, but also by the accuracy of the picture which it probably gives of an individual experience."—*The Month.*

The Infallibility of the Pope. A Lecture. 8vo. 1s.

"A splendid lecture, by one who thoroughly understands his subject, and in addition is possessed of a rare power of language in which to put before others what he himself knows so well."—*Universe.* "There are few writers so well able to make things plain and intelligible as the author of ' The Comedy of Convocation.'. . . The lecture is a model of argument and style."—*Register.*

Reply to the Bishop of Ripon's Attack on the Catholic Church. 6d.

The Harmony of Anglicanism. Report of a Conference on Church Defence. 2s. 6d.

" ' Church Defence' is characterised by the same caustic irony, the same good-natured satire, the same logical acuteness which distinguished its predecessor, the ' Comedy of Convocation.' . . . A more scathing bit of irony we have seldom met with."—*Tablet.* " Clever, humorous, witty, learned, written by a keen but sarcastic observer of the Establishment, it is calculated to make defenders wince as much as it is to make all others smile."—*Nonconformist.*

Marshalliana—The above 5 pamphlets in one volume, 426 pages, 8vo., published at 10s. in paper covers, now offered for 6s. in cloth.

Holy Places; their Sanctity and Authenticity. By the Rev. Fr. Philpin. With Maps. Crown 8vo. 6s.; cheap edition, 2s. 6d.

"Fr. Philpin weighs the comparative value of extraordinary, ordinary, and natural evidence, and gives an admirable summary of the witness of the early centuries regarding the holy places of Jerusalem, with archæological and architectural proofs. It is a complete treatise of the subject."—*Month.* "The author treats his subject with a thorough system, and a competent knowledge."—*Church Herald.*

### Dramas, Comedies, Farces. (*See* also page 26.)

Bluebeard; or, the Key of the Cellar. Drama in 3 Acts. *Children.* 6d.

The Violet Sellers. Drama in Three Acts. *Children.* 6d.

Whittington and his Cat. Drama in Nine Scenes. *Children.* 6d.

St. Eustace. A Drama in Five Acts. *Male.* 1s.

St. William of York. A Drama in Two Acts. *Male.* 6d.

He would be a Lord. Comedy in Three Acts. *Male.* 2s.

He would be a Soldier. Comedy in 2 Acts. *Male.* 6d.

The Enchanted Violin. Comedy in Two Acts. *Male.* 6d.

Finola. An Opera, from Moore's Melodies, in Four Acts. 1s.

Shandy Maguire. A Farce in Two Acts. *Male.* 2s.

The Duchess Transformed. A Comedy in One Act. By W. H. A. *Female.* 6d.

The Reverse of the Medal. A Drama in Four Acts. *Female.* 6d.

Ernscliff Hall: or, Two Days Spent with a Great-Aunt. A Drama in Three Acts. *Female.* 6d.

Filiola. A Drama in Four Acts. *Female.* 6d.

The Secret. Drama in One Act. By Mrs. Sadlier. *Female.* 1s.

The Convert Martyr; or, Dr. Newman's "Callista," dramatised by Dr. Husenbeth. 2s.

Shakespeare. Tragedies and Comedies. Expurgated edition for Schools. By Rosa Baughan. 6s. Comedies, in a separate volume, 3s. 6d.

---

Road to Heaven. A game for family parties, 1s. & 2s.

# R. WASHBOURNE'S
## Catalogue of Books from America.

|  | s. | d. |
|---|---|---|
| **Adventures of a Captain.** By Lady Blanche Murphy | 4 | 0 |
| **Adventures of a Casquet, The.** 2s. 6d., superior edition | 4 | 0 |
| **African Fabiola** | 6 | 0 |
| **Alba's Dream,** and other Stories | 6 | 0 |
| **Alice Harmon,** and other Tales. By an "Exile of Erin" | 5 | 0 |
| **All for Love;** or, from the Manger to the Cross | 8 | 0 |
| **Alzog's Church History.** 3 vols. | 60 | 0 |
| **Amulet, The.** By Conscience | 4 | 0 |
| **Anecdotes, Catholic.** By Mrs. J. Sadlier. 3 vols. | 11 | 0 |
| **Angel Guide;** or, Year of First Communion | 3 | 6 |
| **Anthony;** or, the Silver Crucifix | 2 | 6 |
| **Apostleship of Prayer.** By Rev. H. Ramière | 6 | 0 |
| **Apostolic, An, Woman;** Sister Francis Xavier | 10 | 0 |
| **Ars Rhetorica.** Auctore R. P. Martino du Cygne | 3 | 0 |
| **Assunta Howard,** and other Stories and Sketches | 6 | 0 |
| **Barbara Leigh.** A Christmas Sketch. By A. L. S. | 3 | 0 |
| **Beauties of the Catholic Church.** By Fr. Shadler | 8 | 0 |
| **Bertha;** or, The Consequence of a Fault. 2s. 6d. and | 4 | 0 |
| **Better Part, The.** A Tale from Real Life | 2 | 6 |
| **Bible.** Large 4to., morocco elegant, with clasps | 72 | 0 |
| **Bible.** 4to., cloth, 21s.; French morocco, 27s. 6d.; morocco | 34 | 0 |
| **Bible.** 8vo., cloth, 8s.; persian calf, 21s.; morocco | 25 | 0 |
| **Bible.** 18mo., cloth, 6s.; roan, 7s.; persian calf 8s. & 9s.; morocco, 11s. 6d. & 18s.; calf | 20 | 0 |
| **Bible History for the Use of Catholic Schools.** By a Teacher. Illustrated | 5 | 0 |
| **Bible History for the Use of Schools.** By Bishop Gilmour. Illustrated | 2 | 0 |
| **Blanche de Marsilly.** An Episode of the Revolution | 2 | 6 |
| **Blessed Virgin in North America, Devotion to.** By Fr. Macleod | 5 | 0 |
| **Blessed Virgin, Life of the.** By Rt. Rev. A. P. Dupanloup, and others. Illustrated | 10 | 0 |
| **Burgomaster's Daughter** (*Strange*) | 2 | 6 |
| **Burke's Sermons and Lectures.** 3 vols. | 30 | 0 |
| **Butler's Lives of the Saints.** 4 vols., 36s.; gilt 40s.; or, bound in 2 vols., 28s.; gilt | 36 | 0 |
| *See* **Lives of the Saints** | | |
| **Cahill's Sermons and Lectures** | 12 | 0 |
| **Captain Rougemont;** or, the Miraculous Conversion | 2 | 6 |
| **Cassilda;** or, The Moorish Princess of Toledo | 2 | 6 |

|  | s. | d. |
|---|---|---|
| **Catholic Keepsake.** A Gift Book for all Seasons ... | 5 | 0 |
| **Catholic Youth's Library,** 6 vols. ... ... ... | 12 | 0 |
| Or separately ; Mysterious Beggar, 2s.. ; The Recluse, 2s. ; The Two Brothers, 2s. ; Young Flower Maker, 2s. ; The Leper's Son, 2s. ; The Dumb Boy, 2s. | | |
| **Catholicity in the Carolinas and Georgia.** By Fr. O'Connell | 12 | 0 |
| **Christ in His Church** ; Businger's Church History, translated by Rev. R. Brennan. Illustrated ... ... ... | 9 | 0 |
| **Christian Life and Vocation.** By Rev. J. Berthier ... | 5 | 0 |
| **Christian Mother.** From the German of Rev. W. Cramer | 3 | 0 |
| **Christian Truths.** Lectures by Rt. Rev. Bishop Chatard | 6 | 0 |
| **Christmas for our dear Little Ones, The First.** Illustrated | 6 | 0 |
| **Church and Moral World.** By Rev. A. J. Thébaud, S.J.... | 15 | 0 |
| **Church and the Gentile World.** By the same. 3 vols. ... | 24 | 0 |
| **Church History.** 1 By Alzog, 3 vols., 60s. 2 By Darras, 4 vols., 48s. 3 By Businger, 9s. 4 By Brennan, 4s. 6d. | | |
| **Commandments of God.** By Rev. M. Müller ... ... | 10 | 0 |
| **Communion, Holy.** By Hubert Lebon ... ... ... | 4 | 0 |
| **Conscience's Works,** 8 vols. ... ... ... ... | 32 | 0 |
| The Amulet, 4s. ; The Conscript and Blind Rosa, 4s. ; Count Hugo, 4s. ; The Fisherman's Daughter, 4s. ; Happiness of Being Rich, 4s. ; Ludovic and Gertrude, 4s. ; The Village Innkeeper, 4s. ; The Young Doctor, 4s. | | |
| **Conscript and Blind Rosa.** By Conscience ... ... | 4 | 0 |
| **Consequence of a Fault** (*Bertha*). 2s. 6d. superfine edition | 4 | 0 |
| **Convert, The** : Leaves from My Experience. By Brownson | 8 | 0 |
| **Cook Book for Lent** (suited to all Seasons of the Year) ... | 1 | 0 |
| **Counsels for each Day in the Week** (*Friendly*) ... ... | 0 | 6 |
| **Count Hugo, of Graenhove.** By Conscience ... ... | 4 | 0 |
| **Crasset's Devout Meditations**... ... ... ... | 8 | 0 |
| **Crown of Heaven, The.** From the German of Stoeger ... | 6 | 0 |
| **Crown of Thorns, Mystery of.** By a Passionate Father ... | 5 | 0 |
| **Dalaradia** ; or, The Days of King Milcho. By W. Collins | 4 | 0 |
| **Darras's Church History.** 4 vols. ... ... ... | 48 | 0 |
| **Divine Paraclete.** Sermons. By Rev. T. S. Preston ... | 5 | 0 |
| **Divine Sanctuary, The.** By the Rev. T. S. Preston ... | 4 | 0 |
| **Divinity of Christ, The.** By Rt. Rev. Dr. Rosecrans ... | 2 | 6 |
| **Dumb Boy** (*Catholic Youth*) ... ... ... ... | 2 | 0 |
| **Dupont (Léon Papin.) Life of** (*Holy Man of Tours*) ... | 6 | 0 |
| **Ecclesiastical Law, Elements of.** By Rev. S. B. Smith, D.D. | 20 | 0 |
| ,, ,, Vol. 2, **Ecclesiastical Trials** ... ... | 18 | 0 |
| **Emerald Gems.** Irish Fireside Tales ... ... ... | 6 | 0 |
| **Epistles and Gospels, Explanation of.** By Goffine ... | 9 | 0 |

|   | s. | d. |
|---|---|---|
| **Ethel Hamilton.** By Anna T. Sadlier | 3 | 0 |
| **Eucharist (Holy) and Penance.** By Rev. M. Müller | 8 | 0 |
| **European Civilization, Protestantism and Catholicity Compared.** By Balmes | 12 | 0 |
| **Evidences of Catholicity.** By Archbishop Spalding | 10 | 6 |
| **Evidences of Religion.** By L. Jouin, S.J. | 6 | 0 |
| **Faith of Our Fathers, The.** By Rev. Archbishop Gibbons | 4 | 0 |
| Cheap edition, in paper covers, 2s. | | |
| **Father Oswald.** A Genuine Catholic Story | 4 | 0 |
| **Fickle Fortune.** A Story of Place La Grève | 4 | 0 |
| **First Communicants, Instructions for.** By Dr. Schmitt | 2 | 6 |
| **First Communicant, Little.** (*Life's Happiest Day*) | 4 | 0 |
| **First Communion (My).** From the German of Fr. Buchmann | 4 | 0 |
| **First Communion, Year of.** (*Angel Guide*) | 3 | 6 |
| **Fisherman's Daughter, The.** By Conscience | 4 | 0 |
| **Fisherman's Daughter.** Translated by Mrs. Monroe | 4 | 0 |
| **Four Seasons, The.** By Rev. J. W. Vahey | 4 | 0 |
| **Francis Xavier (St.), Life of.** From the Italian of Bartoli | 8 | 0 |
| **Friendly Voice**; or, the Daily Monitor | 0 | 6 |
| **Future of Catholic Peoples.** By Baron de Haulleville | 6 | 0 |
| **Genius of Christianity.** By Chateaubriand | 10 | 6 |
| **Gertrude (St.) Manual**; or Spirit of Devotion, 504 pages | 4 | 0 |
| **God our Father.** By a Father of the Society of Jesus | 4 | 0 |
| **God the Teacher of Mankind.** By Rev. M. Müller : Holy Eucharist and Penance, 8s. The Greatest and the First Commandment | 10 | 0 |
| **Goffine's Epistles and Gospels** | 9 | 0 |
| **Golden Sands.** First and Second Series, each | 4 | 0 |
| **Great-Grandmother's Secret, The.** 2s. 6d., superior edition | 4 | 0 |
| **Greetings to the Christ Child.** Illustrated | 4 | 0 |
| **Gretchen's Gift**; or, A Noble Sacrifice. By A. I. S. | 3 | 0 |
| **Guardian Angel, Memoirs of a.** By the Abbé Chardon | 4 | 0 |
| **Happiness of Being Rich.** By Conscience | 4 | 0 |
| **Happiness of Heaven.** By a Father of the Society of Jesus | 4 | 0 |
| **Hill's Elements of Philosophy.** 2 vols. | 12 | 0 |
| **History, Compendium of.** By Kerney | 5 | 0 |
| **Holy Man of Tours**; or, the Life of Léon Papin-Dupont | 6 | 0 |
| **Idols**; or, The Secret of the Rue Chaussée d'Antin | 6 | 0 |
| **Indian Sketches.** By Rev. P. J. De Smet, S.J. | 2 | 6 |
| **Intellectual Philosophy.** By Rev. J. De Concilio | 8 | 0 |
| **Invitation Heeded.** By James Kent Stone | 6 | 0 |
| **Irish Faith in America.** Recollections of a Missionary | 4 | 0 |
| **Irish Fireside Tales** (*Emerald*) | 6 | 0 |
| **Irish Martyrs and Confessors, Lives of.** By Myles O'Reilly; and History of the Penal Laws. By Rev. R. Brennan | 12 | 0 |

|  | s. | d. |
|---|---|---|
| **Irish Race (The) Past and the Present.** By Fr. Thébaud | 10 | 0 |
| **Jesuits! The.** By Paul Feval | 3 | 6 |
| **Joint Venture, The**; a Tale in Two Lands | 5 | 0 |
| **Kerney's Compendium of History** | 5 | 0 |
| **King's Page, The,** and other Stories. By Anna T. Sadlier | 3 | 0 |
| **Knowledge and Love of Jesus Christ.** St. Jure, 3 vols. | 31 | 6 |
| **LEO XIII., Life and Acts of.** With a Sketch of the Last Days of Pius IX. Edited by Rev. J. E. Keller, S.J. Illustrated | 6 | 0 |
| **Leper's Son** (*Catholic Youth's*) | 2 | 0 |
| **Letters of a Young Irishwoman to her Sister** | 6 | 0 |
| **Life of our Lord and the Blessed Virgin.** By Rev. R. Brennan. Large 4to., illustrated, half-morocco | 54 | 0 |
| **Life's Happiest Day.** By author of "Golden Sands" | 4 | 0 |
| **Liguori (St.) Life of** | 10 | 0 |
| **Literature, Student's Handbook of British and American.** By Rev. O. L. Jenkins | 10 | 6 |
| **Little Lives of Great Saints.** Illustrated | 5 | 0 |
| **Little Rose of the Sacred Heart** | 2 | 6 |
| **Little Saint of Nine Years.** From French of Mgr. de Segur | 2 | 0 |
| **Little Orator,** and other Tales | 1 | 0 |
| **Little Treatise on the Little Virtues.** By Fr. Roberti, S.J. | 2 | 0 |
| **Little Treatise on Little Sufferings** | 1 | 6 |
| **Lives of the Saints.** By Butler. 4 vols., 8vo., 36s.; gilt, 40s.; or bound in 2 vols., 8vo., 28s.; gilt | 36 | 0 |
| **Lives of the Saints for every Day in the Year.** By Rev. F. X. Weninger, S.J. Illustrated | 50 | 0 |
| **Lives of the Saints, Pictorial,** with Reflection for Every Day | 15 | 0 |
| **Lives of Patron Saints.** Illustrated (*Patron*) | 10 | 0 |
| **Louisa Kirkbride.** By Fr. Thébaud. Illustrated | 10 | 0 |
| **Louise Lateau. A Visit to Bois d'Haine.** By F. Howe | 6 | 0 |
| **Ludovic and Gertrude.** By Conscience | 4 | 0 |
| **Maidens of Hallowed Names** | 4 | 6 |
| **Maddalena;** The Orphan of the Via Media | 4 | 0 |
| **Marcella.** A True Story. 2s. 6d., superior edition | 4 | 0 |
| **Margaret Mary (Blessed), Letters of** (*Sacred Heart*) | 3 | 0 |
| **Marriage, Sure Way to a Happy.** By Fr. Taylor | 4 | 0 |
| **Mary, The Knowledge of.** By Rev. J. de Concilio | 6 | 0 |
| **Mass (The). History of.** By Rev. J. O'Brien | 8 | 0 |
| **Mass (The). The Holy Sacrifice for the Living and the Dead.** By Michael Müller, C.SS.R. | 10 | 0 |
| **Meditations, Devout.** By Crasset. Translated by Dorsey | 8 | 0 |
| **Meditations for Every Day.** By Vercruysse. 2 vols. | 20 | 0 |
| **Miraculous Conversion** (*Captain*) | 2 | 6 |

|  | s. | d. |
|---|---|---|
| **Moorish Princess of Toledo** (*Cassilda*) ... ... ... | 2 | 6 |
| **More** (**Sir Thomas**). By Mrs. Monroe ... ... ... | 6 | 0 |
| **Mother of Washington**, and other Tales. ... ... | 1 | 0 |
| **Muard, Life of Rev. M. J. B.** By Rt. Rev. Dom Robot, O.S.B. | 6 | 0 |
| **Mysterious Beggar** (*Catholic Youth's*) ... ... ... | 2 | 0 |
| **Names that Live in Catholic Hearts** ... ... ... | 4 | 6 |
| **Neptune, The, at the Golden Horn.** Illustrated... ... | 4 | 6 |
| **New Year Greetings.** By St. Francis de Sales ... ... | 1 | 0 |
| **Noethen's Church History** ... ... ... ... | 8 | 0 |
| **Novitiate, Souvenir of the** ... ... ... ... | 4 | 0 |
| **O'Mahony, The, Chief of the Comeraghs.** A Tale of '98... | 6 | 0 |
| **Only a Waif.** By R. A. Braendle ('Pips') ... ... | 4 | 0 |
| **Orphan of Alsace** ... ... ... ... ... | 2 | 6 |
| **Orphan of Moscow.** By Mrs. Sadlier ... ... ... | 3 | 0 |
| **Paradise of God**: or, the Virtues of the Sacred Heart ... | 4 | 0 |
| **Paradise on Earth** ... ... ... ... ... | 2 | 6 |
| **Pastoral Medicine.** Capellmann. Trans. by Rev. W. Dassel | 6 | 0 |
| **Patron Saints.** By E. A. Starr. Illustrated ... ... | 10 | 0 |
| **Paulists' Sermons**: Five Minutes, 1864, 1865, 1871, each... | 6 | 0 |
| **Pearl among the Virtues, The.** By Rev. P. A. De Doss, S.J. | 3 | 0 |
| **Pedro's Daughter** (*King's*) ... ... ... ... | 3 | 0 |
| **Perico the Sad**; or, the Alvareda Family, and other Stories | 6 | 0 |
| **Philomena (St.), Life and Miracles of** ... ... ... | 2 | 6 |
| **Philosophy, Elements of**, comprising Logic and General Principles of Metaphysics. By Rev. Fr. Hill, S.J. ... | 6 | 0 |
| **Philosophy, Ethics, or Moral.** By W. H. Hill, S.J. ... | 6 | 0 |
| **Pius IX., Last Days of.** By Rev. J. E. Keller, S.J. ... | 6 | 0 |
| **Priest of Auvrigny, The**, etc. ... ... ... ... | 2 | 6 |
| **Protestant Reformation.** By Archbishop Spalding. 2 vols., 21s. Cheap edition in 1 vol. ... ... ... | 14 | 0 |
| **Protestant Reformation, &c.** By Rev. T. S. Preston ... | 4 | 0 |
| **Protestant and Catholic Civilization Compared** (*Future*) | 6 | 0 |
| **Raphaela.** By Mlle. Monniot ... ... ... ... | 6 | 0 |
| **Ravignan (Fr.), S. J., Life of.** By Fr. de Ponlevoy ... | 12 | 0 |
| **Recluse, The** (*Catholic Youth's*) ... ... ... | 2 | 0 |
| **Religious, The.** By Rev. J. B. St. Jure. 2 vols. ... | 18 | 0 |
| **Repertorium Oratoris Sacri**: Outlines of 600 Sermons. 4 vols. | 52 | 6 |
| **Richard**; or, Devotion to the Stuarts, 2s. 6d. superior edition | 4 | 0 |
| **Rituale Romanum.** The beautiful 8vo. edition printed by Murphy, of Baltimore. Paper, 16s.; morocco ... | 25 | 0 |
| **Rosary, The, and the Five Scapulars.** By Rev. M. Müller | 6 | 0 |
| **Sacred Chant, Manual of.** By Fr. Mohr ... ... | 2 | 6 |
| **Sacred Heart, Devotions to.** By Rev. S. Franco, S.J. ... Cheap edition, in paper covers, 2s. | 4 | 0 |
| **Sacred Heart, Devotions to** (*Little*) ... ... ... | 2 | 0 |

|  | s. | d. |
|---|---|---|
| Sacred Heart, Hours with ... ... ... ... | 2 | 0 |
| Sacred Heart, Manual. By Fr. Schouppe ... ... | 1 | 6 |
| Sacred Heart, Pearls from the Casquet of ... ... | 3 | 0 |
| Sacred Heart, Virtues of. By Père Boudreaux, S.J. ... | 4 | 0 |
| Sally Cavanagh. By J. C. Kickham ... ... ... | 4 | 6 |
| Sanctuary Boy's Illustrated Manual ... ... ... | 7 | 0 |
| Scapulars (Five), The Devotion of. By Rev. M. Müller ... | 6 | 6 |
| Sermon at the Month's Mind of Most Rev. Abp. Spalding | 1 | 0 |
| Sermons, Repertorium Oratoris Sacri. 4 vols. ... | 52 | 6 |
| Sermons. Divine Paraclete. By Rev. T. S. Preston ... | 5 | 0 |
| Sermons. By the Paulists, 1864, 1865, 1871. Five Minutes, each ... ... ... ... ... ... | 6 | 0 |
| Sermons and Lectures. By Father Burke, O.P. 3 vols. | 30 | 0 |
| Sermons, Lectures, and Discourses. By Bp. Spalding ... | 6 | 0 |
| Sermons, One Hundred Short. By Rev. Fr. Thomas ... | 12 | 0 |
| Sermons on Our Lord, the B.V.M., and Moral Subjects. By Cardinal Wiseman. 2 vols. ... ... ... | 16 | 0 |
| Sermons (53), Preached in the Albany County Penitentiary. By Rev. T. Noethen ... ... ... | 5 | 0 |
| Sermons, Lectures, &c., of Rev. Dr. D. W. Cahill ... | 10 | 0 |
| Sermons or Lectures. By B. Chatard (*Christian Truths*) | 6 | 0 |
| Seton, Mgr., Essays on various subjects, chiefly Roman ... | 8 | 0 |
| Seton, Mrs., Foundress of the Order of Sisters of Charity ... ... ... ... ... ... | 8 | 0 |
| Signs and Ceremonies, Teaching Truth by. Illustrated ... | 6 | 0 |
| Sisters of Charity, Manual of ... ... ... ... | 4 | 0 |
| Six Sunny Months, and other Stories ... ... ... | 6 | 0 |
| Society of Jesus, History of. By Daurignac ... ... | 10 | 0 |
| Spalding (Archbishop), Life of ... ... ... ... | 10 | 6 |
| Spalding's (Abp.) Works. 5 vols. ... ... ... | 52 | 6 |
| Or separately : Evidences of Catholicity, 10s. 6d. Miscellanea, 2 vols., 21s. ; Protestant Reformation, 2 vols., 21s. | | |
| Spiritual Man, The. By the Rev. J. B. Saint-Jure, S.J. ... | 7 | 0 |
| Strange Village ... ... ... ... ... | 2 | 6 |
| Stray Leaves from a Passing Life, and other Stories ... | 6 | 0 |
| Teresa (St.), Thoughts of, for every day in the Year ... | 2 | 6 |
| Thalia; or, Arianism and the Council of Nice. An Historical Tale of the Fourth Century. By the Abbé A. Bayle ... | 6 | 0 |
| Theologia Moralis S. Alphonsi Compendium. Auctore A. Konings, C.SS.R. 24s. 2 vols. in 1, half-morocco ... | 30 | 0 |
| Thesaurus Biblicus; or, Handbook of Scripture Reference | 25 | 0 |
| Thomas Aquinas (St.) Life of ... ... ... ... | 4 | 0 |
| Thomas's One Hundred Short Sermons ... ... | 12 | 0 |
| Truce of God. A Tale of the XI. Century. By Miles ... | 4 | 0 |
| True Faith of our Forefathers ... ... *nett* | 3 | 0 |
| True Men as We Need Them. By Rev. B. O'Reilly ... | 10 | 6 |

26    *R. Washbourne's American Publications.*

|  | s. | d. |
|---|---|---|
| **Twelve Sisters.** By Aunt Fanny. 12 vols. | 15 | 0 |
| Or separately: Bertha's Book, Lucy's Book, Celia's Book, Katie's Book, Helen's Book, Agnes' Book, Mary's Book, Teresa's Book, Rosie's Book, Maggie's Book, Lizzie's Book, Baby's Book, each | 2 | 0 |
| **Two Brothers** (*Catholic Youth's Library*) | 2 | 0 |
| **Ubaldo and Irene.** By Fr. Bresciani, S.J. 2 vols. | 16 | 0 |
| **Vacation Days.** By author of "Golden Sands" | 4 | 0 |
| **Village Innkeeper, The.** By Conscience | 4 | 0 |
| **Village Steeple, The.** A Tale | 2 | 6 |
| **Vincent's (St.) Manual** | 4 | 0 |
| **Visits to the Blessed Sacrament** (*Friendly*) | 0 | 6 |
| **Vows, Catechism of.** By Cotel | 3 | 0 |
| **What Catholics do not Believe.** By Bishop Ryan | 1 | 0 |
| **Wiseman's (Cardinal) Essays.** 6 vols. | 36 | 0 |
| **Wiseman's (Cardinal) Sermons on Our Lord and B. V. M., and Moral Subjects.** 2 vols. | 16 | 0 |
| **Young Doctor.** By Conscience | 4 | 0 |
| **Young Flower-Maker** (*Catholic Youth's*) | 2 | 0 |
| **Zeal in the Work of the Ministry.** By Abbé Dubois | 10 | 0 |
| **Zita (St.), Life of** | 3 | 0 |
| **Vercruysse's Meditations for Every Day.** 2 vols. | 20 | 0 |

### DRAMAS, etc.

|  | s. | d. |
|---|---|---|
| **Babbler, The.** A Drama in One Act. By Mrs. J. Sadlier. *Male* | 1 | 0 |
| **Christmas Tree.** Drama, One Act (*Mixed*) | 1 | 0 |
| **Double Triumph, The.** Dramatized from the Story of Placidus in the "Martyrs of the Coliseum." By Rev. A. J. O'Reilly. *Male* | 2 | 0 |
| **Elder Brother, The.** A Drama in Two Acts. By Mrs. J. Sadlier. *Male* | 1 | 0 |
| **Invisible Hand, The.** A Drama in Three Acts. *Male* | 1 | 0 |
| **Irish Heroine.** A Drama in 5 Acts. By Rev. J. de Concilio (*Mixed*) | 1 | 0 |
| **Julia;** or, The Gold Thimble. A Drama in One Act. By Mrs. J. Sadlier. *Female* | 1 | 0 |
| **Knights of the Cross, The.** A Sacred Drama in Three Acts. *Male* | 2 | 0 |
| **Laurence and Xystus;** or, the Illustrious Roman Martyrs. A Sacred Drama in Five Acts. *Male* | 2 | 0 |
| **Major John Andre.** An Historical Drama, Five Acts. *Male* | 2 | 0 |
| **Maria Antoinnette.** An Historical Drama. *Female* | 2 | 0 |
| **St. Helena;** or, the Finding of the Holy Cross. A Drama in Three Acts. By Rev. J. A. Bergrath. *Female* | 1 | 6 |
| **St. Louis in Chains.** A Drama in Five Acts. *Male* | 2 | 0 |
| **Sylvia's Jubilee**, and 3 other Dramas for the Young, *cloth* | 6 | 0 |

*For the convenience of purchasers the following books referred to in the previous pages are arranged according to price:*

## 6d.

The Brigand Chief, and other Tales
Now is the Accepted Time, and other Tales
What a Child can Do, and other Tales
Sowing Wild Oats, and other Tales
The Two Hosts, and other Tales
The Lost Children of Mount St. Bernard
The Baker's Boy; or, the Results of Industry
A Broken Chain
Life of Paul Seigneret
Prince and Saviour
Mary Christina of Savoy
Count de Montalembert
Pope Pius IX. By White
The Golden Thought of Queen Beryl; The Brother's Grave
The Rod that Bore Blossoms; Patience and Impatience
Clare's Sacrifice
Nellie Gordon, the Factory Girl
Fairy Tales for Little Children
Schmid's, The Canary Bird
———— The Dove
———— The Inundation
———— The Rose Tree
———— The Water Jug
———— The Wooden Cross
Sir Ælfric, and other Tales
Adolphus; or, the Good Son
Nicholas; or, the Reward of a Good Action
Our Blessed Lady of Lourdes
Various Dramas (see page 19)

## 1s.

Moothoosawmy and other Indian Tales, by Lady Herbert
Emily, Nancy, &c., by Lady Herbert
Two Cousins, &c., by Lady Herbert
Kainer; or, the Usurer's Doom
The Fairy Ching
The Two Friends
Yellow Holly, and other Tales
Tableaux Vivants, and other Tales
Wet Days, and other Tales
The Bells of the Sanctuary
Fatal Consequence of Telling Lies
Tom's Crucifix, and Pat's Rosary
Good for Evil, and Joe Ryan's Repentance
The Old Prayer Book, and Charlie Pearson's Medal
Catherine's Promise, and Norah's Temptation [Picture
Annie's First Prayer, and Only a Schmid's Canary Bird (gilt)
———— Dove (gilt)
———— Inundation (gilt)
———— Rose Tree (gilt)
———— Water Jug (gilt)
———— Wooden Cross (gilt)
St. Patrick
St. Bridget and other Saints of Ireland
Walter Ferrers' School Days
Bertram Eldon
Story of a Paper Knife
Terry O'Flinn
The Village Lily
The Angels and the Sacraments
Fairy Tales for Little Children
Rosalie; or, The Memoirs of a French Child
Sir Ælfric and other Tales
Little Orator, and other Tales
Mother of Washington, and other Tales [Ward
Sir Thomas Maxwell and his Story of an Orange Lodge
Diary of a Confessor of the Faith
Countess Adelstan
Paul Seigneret
Life, Passion, Death, and Resurrection of Our Lord
St. Edmund of Canterbury
Our Lady of Lourdes
The Ever Blessed Virgin
The Victories of Rome
The Infallibility of the Pope
Cardinal Wiseman
Stories for my Children

**Little Books of St. Nicholas.** Tales for Children. By F. B. BICKERSTAFFE DREW. 1s. each. Nos. 1 to 6 are ready.

1. Oremus ; 2. Dominus Vobiscum ; 3. Pater Noster ; 4. Per Jesum Christum ; 5. Veni Creator ; 6. Credo ; 7. Ave Maria ; 8. Ora pro nobis ; 9. Corpus Christi ; 10. Dei Genitrix ; 11. Requiem ; 12. Miserere ; 13. Deo Gratias ; 14. Guardian Angel.

### 1s. 6d.

Agnes Wilmott's History
Kainer ; or, the Usurer's Doom (gilt) [(gilt)
The Angels and the Sacraments
The Fairy Ching (gilt) [Tales
The Golden Thought and other
The Two Friends (gilt)
Tableaux Vivants, and other Tales (gilt) [(gilt)
Yellow Holly, and other Tales
Wet Days and other Tales (gilt)
A Daughter of S. Dominick
Good for Evil, and Joe Ryan's Repentance (gilt) [Lies
The Fatal Consequence of Telling
Annie's First Prayer, and Only a Picture (gilt) [(gilt)
Tom's Crucifix, and Pat's Rosary
Terry O'Flinn     Paul Seigneret

The Old Prayer Book, and Charlie Pearson's Medal (gilt)
Catherine s Promise, and Norah's Temptation (gilt)
Legends of the XIIIth Century. 3 volumes each, 1s. 6d.
The Village Lily (gilt)
Fairy Tales for Little Children
The Memoirs of a French Child
The Feasts of Camelot. 2 vols.
Sir Ælfric and other Tales (gilt)
Last of the Catholic O'Malleys
Margarethe Verflassen
Bible Stories from the Old Test.
Sophia and Eulalie— Catholic Pilgrim's Progress
Cardinal Wiseman
Our Blessed Lady of Lourdes

### 2s.

Walter Ferrers' School Days
The Mission Cross
A Daughter of St. Dominick (gilt)
Bessy ; or, the Fatal Consequences of Telling Lies (gilt)
The Adventures of a Protestant in Search of a Religion
Life in Iceland
To Rome and Back     [(gilt)
Fairy Tales for Little Children

Bible History. Illustrated
Rosalie ; or, the Memoirs of a French Child (gilt)
Last of the Catholic O'Malleys
Keighley Hall, and other Tales
Terry O'Flinn (gilt)
Life of St. Wenefred
Paul Seigneret (gilt)
A Month at Lourdes

### 2s. 6d.

Bobbie and Birdie
Bible Stories from the Old Test.
The Monk of the Monastery of Yuste (Charles V.)
My Golden Days
Little Rose of the Sacred Heart
Cassilda ; or, the Moorish Princess of Toledo
Captain Rougemont ; or, the Miraculous Conversion
Catherine Hamilton
Catherine Grown Older
Simple Tales     [a Fault
Bertha ; or the Consequences of

Farleyes of Farley
Sir Humphrey's Trial
Eagle and Dove
Tales and Sketches
Countess Adelstan     [Terror
Recollections of the Reign of
Story of the Life of St. Paul
Recollections of Card. Wiseman
Prince and Saviour
Venerable Anna Maria Taigi
Father Mathew     Holy Places
Comedy of Convocation
Oxford Undergraduate
Harmony of Anglicanism

## 2s. 6d. (continued).

The Three Wishes
Anthony; or, the Silver Crucifix
The Better Part
Blanche de Marsilly
The Burgomaster's Daughter
The Dumb Boy
Life of St. Zita
Indian Sketches [nicants
Instructions for First Commu-
Great-Grandmother's Secret
The Leper's Son
Marcelle        The Recluse
The Adventures of a Casquet
Life of St. Mary Magdalene
The Mysterious Beggar
The Orphan of Alsace
Life of St. Philomena
The Priest of Auvrigny
Strange Village and other Stories
The Two Brothers
The Village Steeple
The Young Flower Maker
Sister Mary Frances of the Five Wounds

## 3s.

True Wayside Tales   [Authors
Gathered Gems from Spanish
The Battle of Connemara
Industry and Laziness
Catherine Hamilton (gilt)
Catherine Grown Older (gilt)
Rupert Aubray       [(gilt)
Story of Marie and other Tales
Gretchen's Gift
Percy Grange
Chats about the Commandments
Cistercian Legends
Chats about the Rosary
Margarethe Verflassen
Pearl among the Virtues
Barbara Leigh    The Lost Son
Ethel Hamilton
St. Angela Merici

## 3s. 6d.

Out in the Cold World
Jack's Boy
The Conquest of Grenada
The Catholic Pilgrim's Progress
From Sunrise to Sunset
Rest, on the Cross
The Feast of Camelot
Tales from many Lands
Canon Schmid's Tales
Tim O'Halloran's Choice
Tom's Crucifix, and other Tales
Fluffy: a Tale for Boys
The Adventures of a Protestant in Search of a Religion
The Barrys of Beigh
Margarethe Verflassen (gilt)
The Heroine of Vesuvius
Tales and Sketches (gilt)
St. German
St. Francis of Assisi
Stories of Martyr Priests
Legends of the Saints
Stories of the Saints. 1st Series
Stories of the Saints. 2nd Series
Stories of the Saints. 3rd Series
Stories of the Saints. 4th Series
Stories of the Saints. 5th Series
Stories of Holy Lives
Blessed Giovanni Columbini
Sister Mary Cherubina Clare
Gregory Lopez, the Hermit
St. Columbkille
Ven. Canori Mora
The History of the Blessed Virgin
History of the Italian Revolution
Two Years in the Pontifical Zouaves
The Oxford Undergraduate of Twenty Years Ago
Festival Tales
Life in the Cloister
The Jesuits. By Paul Feval

## 4s.

Maidens of Hallowed Names
Adventures of a Casquet
My First Communion
Fisherman's Daughter. By Munroe
Great Grandmother's Secret
Paradise of God
Bertha; or, the Consequence of a Fault
Dalaraida; or, the Days of King Milcho
Life's Happiest Day

## 4s. (continued).

Conscience's, The Amulet
The Young Doctor
The Fisherman's Daughter
Count Hugo
The Conscript and Blind Rosa
The Village Innkeeper
Happiness of Being Rich
Ludovic and Gertrude
Cloister Legends
The Truce of God
The Prussian Spy
Memoirs of a Guardian Angel
Rome and her Captors

Adventures of a Captain
Fickle Fortune
The Four Seasons
Golden Sands. 1st Series
Golden Sands. 2nd Series
Greetings to the Christ Child
God our Father
The King's Page and other Stories
Marcelle. A true story
Only a Waif
Souvenir of the Novitiate
Vacation Days

## 5s.

My Lady at Last
Recollections of a Missionary
The Rose of Venice
The Days of King Milcho
Only a Waif   Eagle and Dove
Father Benvenuto Bambozzi
Limerick Veteran
The Victims of the Mammertine
Albertus Magnus
St. Vincent Ferrer
St. Bernardine of Siena

St. Philip Benizi
St. Veronica Giuliani
St. John of God
Venerable Anna Maria Taigi
Life of Our Lord     [America
Devotion to Our Lady in North
Alice Harmon and other Tales
Bible History. Illustrated
The Joint Venture
Catholic Keepsake
Little Lives of Great Saints

## 6s.

Life of Mother Mary Jacqueline Favre, and others
Life of Sister Claude Simplicienne Fardel, and others
St. Patrick     St. Columba
St. Boniface
Holy Places
Marshalliana
Shakespeare. Expurgated edition
The First Christmas for our dear Little Ones
Sir Thomas More
The Mysterious Castle
Perico the Sad and other Tales
Panegyrics of Father Segneri

The Knowledge of Mary
The O'Mahony
Raphaela
Six Sunny Months and other Stories
Stray Leaves and other Stories
Thalia. An Historical Tale
The Two Brides
Alba's Dream and other Stories
Assunta Howard and other Stories
Emerald Gems
Letters of a Young Irishwoman to her Sister
Louise Lateau

## 6s. 6d., to 48s.

Père Lacordaire, 6s. 6d.
Cardinal Wolsey, 6s. 6d.
The Italian Revolution, 7s. 6d.
Life of St. Francis Xavier, 8s.
Goffine's Explanation of the
Epistles and Gospels. Illustrated. 8s.
Life and Acts of Leo XIII. and Last Days of Pius IX. 8s.
Killed at Sedan, 10s. 6d.

*R. Washbourne's Catalogue.* 31

Lives of the Early Popes, 10s.
The First Religious of the Visitation. 2 vols., 10s.
The First Apostles of Europe. 2 vols., 10s.
St. Patrick. 10s.
Patron Saints. 10s.
Life of St. Ligouri, 10s.
Life of the Blessed Virgin. Illustrated. 10s.
Genius of Christianity. 10s. 6d.
Louisa Kirkbride. 10s. 6d.
True Men as we need them. 10s. 6d.
Albertus Magnus. 10s. 6d.
Sir Thomas More. 10s. 6d.
Catholic Anecdotes. 3 vols., 11s.
Catholic Youth's Library. 6 vols., 12s.

Père Ravignan, 12s.
Lives of Irish Martyrs and Confessors. 12s.
Spalding's Reformation, 14s.
Pictorial Lives of the Saints. 15s.
Twelve Sisters. 12 vols., 15s.
Ubaldo and Irene. 2 vols., 16s
Lives of the Saints for every Day in the Year. 25s.
Butler's Lives of the Saints. 2 vols., 28s., gilt, 36s.
St. Jure's Knowledge and Love of Our Lord. 3 vols., 31s. 6d.
Butler's Lives of the Saints. 4 vols., 32s., gilt, 40s.
Cardinal Wiseman's Essays. 6 vols., 36s.
Darras' Church History. 4 vols., 48s.

## HOLY FAMILY CARD OF MEMBERSHIP.

A BEAUTIFUL DESIGN : All who have seen it admire it, and say Nothing equals it.

*Price 6d., or post free, on a roller, 8d. Twelve copies 4s. 6d., or 5s. post free.*

Medals, 3d., 4d., and 6d. each.

## FIRST COMMUNION CARD.

This is also a very Beautiful Design, and commends itself to all who have seen it. It is also arranged as a Memento of Confirmation.

*Price 1s., or post free, on a roller, 1s. 3d. Twelve copies for 9s., or post free 9s. 6d.*

Medals in Silver, 1s., 2s., and 3s. 6d. each.

## CHILDREN OF MARY CARD.

*Price 9d., or post free, on a roller, 1s.*

Medals, 2d. and 3d. each ; or in Silver, 1s., 1s. 6d., 2s., 3s., 4s., 5s., 6s. 6d., and 10s. 6d. each.

**Child of Mary Manual, 1s.**

*R. Washbourne's COMPLETE Catalogue, post free*
*R. Washbourne's Monthly List, post free.*

# THE CHILD'S PICTURE PRAYER BOOK.

In simple language and in large type, on good paper, beautifully illustrated.

The Contents of the book are Morning Prayers, The Angelus, Grace before and after Meals, Night Prayers, Litany of the Blessed Virgin, The Memorare, Prayers during Holy Mass, Divine Praises, Benediction of the Most Blessed Sacrament, Hymns, De Profundis, and the Rosary for the Dead.

**The illustrations are 16 in number, each occupying a full page.**

The binding is in cloth, with a cover designed expressly for the book, and the price, with the pictures in two tints, is 1s., or in stronger binding, 1s. 6d., or with gold on the side, 2s.; with the pictures in seven colours, 1s. 6d., or in stronger binding, 2s., or with gold on the side, 2s. 6d., and with gilt edges 3s., and with full gilt side 3s. 6d., in French morocco, 3 .6d., or extra gilt 4s., in calf, 5s., or extra gilt, 6s.

# THE LITTLE GARDEN ILLUSTRATED.

Abridged in the Latin, with 16 full-page Illustrations: cloth, 1s., with Epistles and Gospels, 1s. 6d.; roan, 1s. 6d.; French morocco, 2s. ditto, extra gilt, 2s. 6d.; calf or morocco, 3s. 6d.; ditto, extra gilt, 4s. 6d.; with Epistles and Gospels 6d. extra on the above.

# R. WASHBOURNE'S POPULAR EDITION
## OF
# THE GARDEN OF THE SOUL.

This edition of THE GARDEN OF THE SOUL is especially distinguished by bearing the IMPRIMATUR OF THE CARDINAL-ARCHBISHOP OF WESTMINSTER. Amongst the many valuable additions, not before inserted in THE GARDEN OF THE SOUL, will be found the rites of administering the Sacraments in Latin and English, Devotions to the Sacred Heart, Devotion of the Quarant 'Ore, the Prayers for a Journey, or Itinerarium, Devotions to the Angel Guardians, The Way of the Cross, the Devotion of the Bona Mors, and many other devotions, and the Vespers in ordinary use. Especial attention is directed to the excellent paper and bold type used n the edition.

Embossed, 1s.; with rims and clasps, 1s. 6d.; with Epistles and Gospels 1s. 6d.; with rims and clasp, 2s. French morocco, 2s.; with rims and clasps, 2s. 6d.; with Epistles and Gospels, 2s. 6d.; with rims and clasps, 3s. French morocco, extra gilt, 2s. 6d.; with rims and clasp, 3s.; with Epistles and Gospels, 3s.; with rims and clasp, 3s. 6d.

Calf or morocco, 4s., with clasp, 5s. 6d.; extra gilt, 5s., or 6s. 6d. with clasp. Calf or morocco, extra gilt, 5s., with clasp, 6s 6d. Morocco, with two patent clasps, 12s. Morocco antique, with corners and two clasps, 18s. Velvet, with rims and clasp, 8s., 10s. 6d., 13s. Russia, with clasp, 10s., 12s. 6d. Russia antique, with corners and two clasps, 20s. Ivory, with rims and clasp, 12s., 16s., 20s., 22s. 6d.

Any of the above can be had with Epistles and Gospels, 6d. extra

The Epistles and Gospels may be had separately, cloth, 6d., or 4s. 6d. per dozen; roan, 1s. 6d.

www.ingramcontent.com/pod-product-compliance
Lightning Source LLC
Chambersburg PA
CBHW031820230426
43669CB00009B/1204